Ruth Page's
Gardening Journal

Ruth Page's Gardening Journal

RUTH PAGE

Houghton Mifflin Company

BOSTON

1989

For information about permission to reproduce selections from this book,
write to Permissions, Houghton Mifflin Company, 2 Park Street, Boston,
Massachusetts 02108.

Library of Congress Cataloging-in-Publication Data

Page, Ruth W.
Ruth Page's gardening journal.

1. Gardening—Miscellanea.   I. Title.
II. Title: Gardening journal.
SB453.P24   1989   635   88-13743
ISBN 0-395-49339-0
ISBN 0-395-50091-5 (pbk.)

Printed in the United States of America

Q   10   9   8   7   6   5   4   3   2   1

*To Proc, who taught me
how to garden*

ACKNOWLEDGMENTS

Behind *The Gardening Journal* public radio program is a team that, through great effort and enthusiasm, makes the program seem effortless and natural. Likewise, a dedicated, energetic group of people gathered, edited, and embellished the radio scripts so that this book is far more than a collection of three-and-a-half-minute radio programs.

Thanks to illustrator Bonnie Acker, a longtime National Gardening Association member and *Gardening Journal* fan whose vision is a perfect match for ours. There is no match for Bonnie's cheerful spirit.

We are grateful to Houghton Mifflin editor Frances Tenenbaum, who was quick to recognize *The Gardening Journal* as a natural for a book. She was even faster at guiding us through every publishing stage in half the time it takes most books, and without a single hitch.

At the National Gardening Association, Cheryl Dorschner deserves thanks for editing the manuscript and leading both manuscript and art through their various incarnations; Julia Gilbert, for being the superwoman behind every aspect of both the radio program and the book; Charlie Nardozzi, staff horticulturist, for (with a smile) checking facts on demand; and Dolores Spies and Barbara Godfrey, for adeptly juggling our computer files and administrative needs.

Many thanks to editor Susan Littlefield, who played a major role in preparing the manuscript and made sure all our horticultural facts are accurate.

Also sincere thanks to Ev Grimes for her unlimited knowledge of public radio production and her careful editing of radio scripts and tape; Resolution, Inc. for its recording studio and engineer Chris Albertine for his expertise and infinite patience; and the Vermont Public Radio staff, particularly Ray Dilley, Steve Olson, Sam Sanders, and Betty Smith Mastaler, for helping us get the radio series on the air. Last, our deepest gratitude goes to all the public radio stations and many listeners across the country for making *The Gardening Journal* an overwhelming success.

CONTENTS

Acknowledgments   vii

Foreword   xiii

1. THE GARDENING YEAR BEGINS   1

    A Gardener's Resolutions   1

    Catalog Dementia   3

2. STARTING SEEDS INDOORS   7

3. FANTASIES AND FANTASTIC GARDENS   10

    The Romantic Garden   10

    Moon Gardens   12

    Marsh Gardens   14

    Making a Meadow   16

4. REPOTTING HOUSE PLANTS   18

5. SPRING-FLOWERING TREES   21

    Shadblow   21

    Dogwood   23

    Crabapples   25

6. LANDSCAPING AT THE PAGES'   28

7. LESSONS IN BUYING AND PLANTING TREES   31

8. FEEDING THE GOOD EARTH   36

    Compost   36

    Manure   38

x · Contents

Green Manures 40

Supplemental Feedings 43

9. SECRETS TO BUYING TRANSPLANTS 46

10. DRESSING UP THE HOUSE 50

Porch Plants 50

Window Boxes 52

11. OLD-FASHIONED FLOWERS 55

Columbine 55

Foxgloves 57

Dianthus 59

Poppies 61

Sunflowers 62

12. PROBLEM SOLVERS TO THE RESCUE 65

Morning Glories 65

The Goatsbeard Solution 67

Under-Tree Growers 69

13. THE CARROT CAPER 73

14. BEETLES AND OTHER BUGS 76

The Good, the Bad, and the Ugly 76

Flea Beetles 79

Japanese Beetles 81

Slugs 82

15. OLD MOTHER HUBBARD 85

16. VEGETABLE FAVORITES 88

Tastiest Tomatoes 88

Elegant Eggplants 91

Peppers, Sweet and Hot 94

The Perfect Pumpkin 96

17. ONIONS AND LEEKS 100

Contents · xi

18. HELPFUL CREATURES   104

    Praying Mantis   104
    Earthworms   106
    Ladybugs   107
    Honeybees   109

19. PESTICIDES: NATURAL IS NOT ALWAYS SAFE   112

20. PERENNIAL GREATS   115
    Irises   115
    Daylilies   117

21. THE SCENTED GARDEN   119

    Of Scents and Spirits   119
    Geraniums   121
    Old Roses   122
    Lilacs   124

22. GARDENING AS THERAPY   126

23. CRITTER CONTROL   129

    Midnight Raiders   129
    Crows   132

24. CAULIFLOWER   135

25. TRY IT, YOU MAY LIKE IT   138

    Kale   138
    Spinach   139
    Parsnips   141
    Celeriac   143
    Radishes   145

26. BAGGING FOOD CROPS   147

27. SAVING SEEDS   150

28. HARVEST — PICKING AT THE PEAK   153

29. PUTTING FOODS BY 156

   Pickling Cukes 156
   Freezing Corn 158
   Drying Fruits and Vegetables 160

30. HERBS AND POTPOURRI 162

   Drying Herbs 162
   Potpourri 164

31. BULBS FOR FOUR SEASONS 166

   Spring 166
   Summer 171
   Autumn 173
   Winter 174

32. EXTENDING THE SEASON 176

   Frost Protection 176
   Flower Cuttings 178

33. CLOSING DOWN THE GARDEN 181

   Fall Cleanup 181
   Winterizing the Garden 183

34. THE VALUE OF TREES 186

35. THE GARDENER INDOORS 189

   Voilà Violets 189
   Easy as Amaryllis 191
   The Gardenia and the Spider Mites 193
   Christmas Cactus 194

36. WINTER SCENES 197

   About the National Gardening Association 201

FOREWORD

When we began *The Gardening Journal* series back in 1986 on our local Vermont public radio station, our intention was simply to spread the gardening word and bring a smile to the faces of Vermonters as they began or ended their day. We surely didn't realize the full impact of what we were creating.

The National Gardening Association's mission is to provide gardening information nationwide — to people of all generations, regions, and abilities. Our magazine, *National Gardening,* is read by about a half million people each month. With a short daily spot on public radio, we knew we could reach a million people immediately and more in time. Within four months of *The Gardening Journal's* April 1988 national broadcast, more than 130 stations were carrying the series.

Ruth Page was the obvious choice to host the series. She had just retired from her position as editor in chief of our magazine, a post she had held for seven years. I've known Ruth and her wonderful family ever since I came to Vermont, and it's impossible not to be affected by her enthusiasm for gardening and her sparkling attitude toward life. However, I underestimated the devotion her listeners would feel. Overnight, people began changing their routines to catch the program — setting their alarms five or ten minutes earlier so they would be fully awake when it came on. We received calls from listeners all over the country who had missed a program, asking what Ruth had talked about that day. Ruth Page had joined a million families across the United States.

Hearing from the listeners is one of the most rewarding parts of doing our radio series. One of our favorite letters came from a man in Vermont during the first winter of broadcast: "I want you to know how much my wife and I enjoy hearing *The Gardening Journal* at 6:40 each morning. We just have time to get up, feed the fire, wash our faces, start the heat under the coffeepot, and sink into our easy chairs before the program begins. It is a great way to start the day, especially since our garden, clearly visible from our picture window, is under thirty-two inches of snow and it's just a bit early to start anything inside the house as yet." And from a listener in Minnesota: "Your program is my last chance to sit quietly, listen, and sip my coffee before the day explodes into activity. Beginning a day with thoughts of growing things is gentle and inspirational for the spirit."

With *The Gardening Journal* we provide not only gardening advice and commentary but a time for people to contemplate nature and its wisdom and wonders. Every weekday *The Gardening Journal* presents a different view of gardening, from designing a Shakespearean garden to taking a close look at the life of a ladybug.

Since the first month of broadcast, listeners have asked us to collect Ruth's wonderful vignettes in a book. I wish we could have published them all. We've pulled together our listeners' favorites and favorites of our own in a collection that we think speaks of gardening in America, with all its novel ideas, family traditions, laughter, and frustration. We hope that the stories in this book will bring you back to the garden, whether it's under three feet of snow or buried in your childhood. In the end, there is really nothing more important than taking care of the earth and letting it take care of you.

CHARLES SCOTT
President, National Gardening Association

Ruth Page's
Gardening Journal

○ 1 ○

The Gardening
Year Begins

A GARDENER'S RESOLUTIONS

January was named for Janus, a god with two faces, one on each side of his head. That guy didn't trust anybody. I suspect that's because he knew from eons of experience that no one keeps New Year's resolutions, including gardeners who have been working on their list of resolutions since last summer. Here are a few I've made more times than I want to count.

First off, this year we will make a careful, measured vegetable garden plan showing exactly where every single thing is planted, and we'll keep a record of varieties, maturity dates, and performance.

Remember those weedy beans and onions? This year we'll mulch everything thoroughly and save all that back-breaking work.

For three years we've been saying we'd dry the onions well, with their tops on, and braid them. This year, we'll do it.

In spring, we'll till earlier than usual so there'll be time to make raised beds for the greens, carrots, beets, and tomatoes. Then we won't be forever walking on the beds and compacting the soil.

We will turn the compost regularly, we will, we will, we will.

To make sure we plant some crops early and use cover ups, we'll buy the plastic covers in March; once we've invested in them, we know we'll use them.

Too bad we didn't properly prune the two apple trees and the shrubs around the house last year; but this year we'll be sure it's done — we'll put it on the appointment calendar right now.

You see? Any gardener can finish that list easily. Yours may be different, but the idea's the same. The good news is that each year we do accomplish some of the things we've planned. The bad news is that the time we give to those is taken from something else, so next year the list is just as long. Different, maybe, but just as long.

Our resolutions illustrate the triumph of hope over experience. In January, we envision spring and summer as marvelously long — those warm days *are* so much longer than winter's stingy nine-hour days. (Popular songs about the long, lazy hazy days don't help — they sound so spacious.)

Then the real spring and summer come. In Vermont, spring lasts about a week: crocuses, tulips, forsythia, and lilacs all bloom practically at once; trees have buds on Monday and leaves on Wednesday. Nature moves so fast we yearn for an eight-day week to try to catch up.

The typical Vermont summer lasts about thirty days and provides a maximum of two weekends, on one of which it rains.

Once we face facts, we aren't so crushed when we realize in mid-October that we followed one whole batch of resolutions perfectly, but missed another whole batch.

Janus is really the gardener's god. He checks to see what happened last year before planning what to do this year. If there's one thing we're sure of, it's that he has a sense of humor. Any god forced to look at two years in the garden simultaneously couldn't survive without it.

CATALOG DEMENTIA

You can spot real gardeners as easily in January as in July. Bright seed catalogs cover their coffee tables. A couple of catalogs lie on the kitchen table beside the toast and jam. There are a few on the bedside table in case of insomnia. There may even be one or two in the car. These gardeners suffer a mild illness known as catalog dementia.

Real gardeners don't watch TV on a day when a new catalog arrives. They admire its cover; then they feel its crisp, newly printed pages; they bury their noses in it and become deaf to phones and doorbells. Fido, barking to be let in, is wasting his energy.

Getting all the available information from good catalogs takes some skill. How do you choose wisely among seventeen varieties of tomato and fifteen kinds of corn from a dozen or more companies?

Here in the North, the first thing we look for is "days to maturity." No use putting in standard lima beans if your growing season is only one hundred days and you have no greenhouse. If you aren't sure of your area's average last frost date in spring and the first in fall, call your local Cooperative Extension office; they'll know.

Southern gardeners look first for information on disease and pest resistance, since these problems are increased in their climate. Resistant varieties are the first step in problem control. In the catalogs, capital letters following a plant variety name indicate disease resistance. The *V* means it resists verticillium wilt. *F* means it's resistant to one of the fusarium wilts, and so on. Remember, "resistant" does not mean immune. It only means the plant has a strong ability to withstand or repel those infections. A variety the catalog says is tolerant to infection may get the disease, but it will still be able to produce.

Then there's frost tolerance. The catalog will tell you, for example, at what temperature your cucumbers may roll over and play dead, and which tomatoes can shiver a bit and survive. Again, knowing your average last frost date in spring and the average first frost date in fall will help you choose appropriate varieties for your garden.

What about how a plant grows? Is it a bush? A vine? Compact? Spreading? Very tall? People with small gardens and those who plant mostly in containers look for bush varieties. Gardeners with plenty of space often like the big, spreading vines with their broad, green leaves.

More catalogs are stressing flavor these days. They tell which tomato is sweetest, which hot pepper is most pungent, which cucumbers are mildest.

If you plan to save seeds from the garden for future plantings, look for the words "standard" or "open-pollinated" in the catalog. Seeds of such varieties will produce offspring like themselves. With a hybrid, however, you never know what offspring you'll get — it may come forth with the worst faults of both parents. If you've ever had volunteer squash growing in the compost pile, you know this; most of the fruits look like a three-year-old's idea of a petrified amoeba from the deep, dark sea.

Some catalogs give advice on plant culture and harvest. Some even suggest how many seeds you'll need per consumer in the family.

Finally, the catalog tells whether or not seeds have been treated with fungicide. Fungicides give seeds a better chance of germinating when soil is cold and wet. Since some gardeners prefer not to use chemicals in their gardens, many companies offer a choice of treated and untreated seed.

The one thing the catalogs won't do for us is to curb our enthusiasm. I've yet to meet a gardener anywhere who has the self-control to buy just the right amount of seed. At our house we always have seeds left over, and usually save them for the next year. When we remember to do it, we seal up the seeds in their packets and put them in the freezer; when we forget, they languish in the heavy cardboard "seed box" that gets stored in the dry cellar all winter.

Until now we've always planted leftover seeds according to a system my mother would call "by guess and by golly." We say, "Well, these seeds aren't really fresh, so we'll just put out twice as many as the packet suggests. If too many come up, we'll thin them out."

That doesn't work badly, either; we're usually impressed by the good germination of year-old seeds, and have been known to use two-year-old ones. But thinning is no fun, and I hate throwing out innocent little plants that are healthy and doing their best, just because I planted too much seed. That way of handling leftover seeds is just too casual. From now on I think we'll try a germination test with some of the seeds, to learn in advance how well they're going to germinate. Seeds that are clearly still eager to grow we can then plant with a less lavish hand.

The easiest way to check germination is to spread some of the year-old seeds on a very damp paper towel, then put another damp paper towel on top. Roll them up or fanfold them, and put them in a plastic bag. Set it in a warm place like the top of the fridge or the TV. When you unroll the towels a few days later, you'll quickly know whether your corn, peas, or beans from last year are germinating well. If none have germinated, you may have peeked too soon. Or you may have a really old batch. If fewer than half of them germinate, pitch them out; they're not worth the planting effort. You can test small quantities of each variety of seed; while they're germinating, get the garden prepared. Then plant the rest of your leftovers according to what the test showed.

Gardeners, especially those in areas with very cool springs, may want to presprout a number of their current garden seeds for planting. The larger seeds like peas and corn are best for this. Presprouting gives a little head start on the season to crops you don't grow to transplant size indoors. Most seeds need a lot more warmth for germination than the plants will need in order to grow. The warmer the ground, the quicker the germination. Corn, for instance, takes three weeks to germinate if the soil is only 50–55 degrees (it won't germinate at all when soil temperature is below 50). But in your paper towels, in a warm spot, little curly sprouts may appear in three to five days. In the North, presprouted seeds of corn and other crops that like a long, hot summer can make a big difference in the harvest date.

Presprouting isn't a technique that's very handy for anyone with a great big garden; it's too fussy. But for testing seed it's hard to beat. And if you like to plant succession crops after the peas and spinach have gone by, presprouting saves midseason time. Also, in a dry July, you can get away with less watering. If you planted unsprouted seeds, you might have to water them a bit every day to get them to germinate. Your presprouted seeds are past that first hurdle.

———o 2 o———

Starting Seeds Indoors

After some thirty years, I still get a thrill watching seeds poke their green shoots up next to the kitchen or living room windows. That's one reason my husband and I start at least some of our seeds indoors. When our care leads to healthy, vigorous adult plants, we can be justly proud of the harvest of fruits and flowers. Nature didn't do it all alone.

When you grow plants from seeds you have a far wider selection of varieties than if you buy seedlings for transplanting. After growing ordinary varieties for a time, it's fun to try new ones you've spotted in catalogs, like Chocolate Bell peppers, Mexican Ribbed stuffing tomatoes, Vita Sweet carrots, Moon and Stars watermelon, or the latest thing in pansies, petunias, or portulaca. Often, in trying something new, you want to start its seeds indoors. You can certainly control the environment better than whoever's responsible for our weather.

Choosing containers is easy; just be sure yours are at least two or three inches deep, so roots will have growing space. Peat pots, plastic foam cups, clay pots, and yogurt containers are all excellent. They're better than big pots or flats, because in those the plant roots tangle with each other and are hard to separate when you transplant.

Make drainage holes in each of your containers, if they don't already have them. With plastic cups, I usually poke about four pencil-point holes around the edge, right near the bottom of the cup. Peat pots don't require holes, but remember that the peat absorbs moisture, so as seeds grow watch water levels carefully.

Don't put garden soil in your containers. You need a light, weed-free, disease-free mix that won't form a crust on top. What provides all this? A soilless mix. You can buy the mix or make your own: one part vermiculite, one part perlite, and one part peat. Most, but not all, purchased mixes have some fertilizer in them; the homemade mix does not. If your mix is unfertilized, once the true leaves (second set) unfold, add a little liquid fertilizer diluted to one-eighth strength every other watering.

Moisten your planting mix well before putting in the seeds, then move the pots to a warm place to speed germination.

To maintain moisture without overdoing it, wrap each batch of pots in clear plastic to make little greenhouses. If you don't use plastic coverings, keep the planting medium moist, but never wet, and make sure pots can drain. Once the seedlings emerge, take off the plastic and move the trays to bright, sunny windows or place under fluorescent lights for at least twelve to sixteen hours a day.

Plants must have adequate light or they'll get tall, weak, and spindly and be hard to transplant. It's tricky to get adequate window light. At my house we use two long-bar fluorescent lights hung two to four inches above the plant trays, moving the lights up as the plants grow. We leave lights on for sixteen hours for the first week or two, then for about twelve hours. We usually turn the plant lights off when we start thinking about bedtime tooth brushing, and on again after breakfast in the morning; that makes it part of our routine and easier to remember.

Light works together with temperature to keep plants from getting leggy. Most seedlings prefer temperatures of sixty-five to seventy degrees Fahrenheit in the daytime and around fifty-five at night.

If you've never started seeds, don't worry too much about it. Remember, nature has designed them to *want* to grow. You and the garden seeds have exactly the same goal — what could be more reassuring?

—— ∘ 3 ∘ ——

Fantasies and Fantastic Gardens

THE ROMANTIC GARDEN

Now and then I wake up in the middle of the night and can't get back to sleep. It's the perfect time to indulge in one of my favorite horticultural pursuits — picturing my fantasy garden. Like my fantasy house, it comes with plenty of help — devoted workers who wouldn't dream of letting a tendril of creeping Charlie or a blade of Johnsongrass invade the velvet lawn.

Probably every gardener has a dream landscape, a landscape made of memories of gorgeous gardens seen in travels, stunning pictures from gardening books, and a good dose of imagination.

Our fantasy gardens say a lot about our personalities. Practical types with well-organized minds no doubt dream of neatly ordered rows of vegetables, elegant European lettuces, delicate French haricots verts, vivid red stalks of Swiss chard.

Those with an engineering bent probably fantasize about rows of apple trees neatly espaliered against fences, carrying their rosy fruits in precisely ordered ranks. The favorite flower of this kind of gardener is probably the tulip.

The meditative mind may muse on the simplicity and serenity of a Japanese garden, every stone and plant placed with much forethought to produce flowing color, delicate texture, and striking line.

One garden I like to imagine is old-fashioned and romantic. It's full of lush, colorful borders of perennials (all in full bloom all season long and perfectly cared for by my fantasy gardeners). Its focal point and crowning glory is a gazebo. Flowering vines tumble across it, twining up the posts and over the roof. Inside, surrounded by wicker chairs with plump cushions, stands a table draped in white linen, on which sits an elegant tea — dainty sandwiches, lacy cookies, sparkling silver, and flowery china. I, in my typical blue jeans and pink T-shirt, am nowhere to be seen; but in the background, sniffing a perfect rose, is a lady in a long white gown, twirling a rose-pink parasol.

Of course this is utterly out of character for me, and outrageously beyond the bounds of possibility, but I really would like to have a gazebo at the center of my garden. I'd also love a place where I can sit and have nothing to do but gaze at the plants nodding in the summer breeze.

So there's my dream garden, rich in trees, flowering shrubs, curling vines of kiwi and cucumber, climbing rose and trumpeting morning glory; vegetable, fruit, and ornamental plants together making a perfect tapestry of color and shape.

My imaginary gardeners, of course, are in the various sheds and greenhouses getting succession plants ready to set out. I love knowing I can work with them whenever I have time, and also knowing the garden won't suffer if I need some time out. Ah, me — I can dream, can't I?

MOON GARDENS

To call it an all-white garden makes it sound a little bland; but call it a "moon garden" and it sounds intriguing and beautiful. And when carefully planned, it is. A moon garden is ideal for people who work late and can enjoy the garden only when the light is fading. It's also a perfect place to entertain when guests arrive after sundown. As twilight deepens, all your colorful plants look black or gray; but the whites still stand out.

Whites look their best in late evening. They not only remain visible, they take on an added glow when there's no glaring sun to outshine them. Of course, a garden of white flowers is not *just* for evening enjoyment, because even white needn't be monochromatic. There are choices: the clear, pure white of candytuft; the creamy ivory of some of the astilbes; the greenish white of that delicate wildflower, Solomon's seal; and the pale yellowish white of some irises. Many white flowers have contrasting colors as accents. White Shasta daisies (*Chrysanthemum* × *superbum*) have bright yellow centers; the elegant Imperial Silver lily (*Lilium* 'Imperial Silver Strain') is dotted with delicate vermilion specks; and a rose-colored eye winks from among the pure white petals of Everest phlox (*Phlox paniculata* 'Everest'). All the whites, of course, have foliage in varying shades of green, so you get handsome daytime contrasts.

Differences in texture and shape are also eye-catching — the airy froth of baby's breath (*Gypsophila*) against the chubby pompoms of a white chrysanthemum, or the feathery spires of astilbe against the dense snowball heads of phlox. Spires of white delphinium can contrast with a cascade of scalloped white petunia blossoms. When you add to your garden palette the various shades in the foliage of these plants, including those with gray-green, yellow-green, and variegated leaves, you needn't fear there will be any boring expanses of white.

My favorite moon garden plant is the white peony. Peonies have a fairly short flowering period, but when they're in bloom they're spectacular. They're also long-lived and trouble-free, and have pretty foliage throughout the season. I prefer the single peonies, especially the cultivar 'Krinkled White', whose pure white petals are set off by golden stamens.

White Siberian iris is also beautiful; a clump of *Iris sibirica* 'Snow Queen', the white blossoms hovering like a cloud of butterflies above the grassy foliage, takes your breath away. Siberian iris is long-lived and will grow even in moist areas.

Perhaps because they remind me of English cottage gardens, or maybe because of their quaint name, I like foxgloves. The moon gardener will want *Digitalis purpurea* 'Alba', its four-foot spires lined with dainty, ivory-white, bell-shaped blossoms. This is a biennial, so each plant will produce only leaves the first season, then flower and die the second year. But in light shade, with rich, highly organic soil, the plants often self-sow.

What about white flowers that offer a delicious scent? The annual flowering tobacco, nicotiana, is a good choice. Available in pure white, as well as in other colors, its flowers are especially fragrant at night. And what moon garden could do without the moonflower vine (*Ipomoea alba*), an annual whose five-inch blossoms open at night to scent the evening air?

You can visit your moon garden at day's end to relax, inhale the scents, and admire the quiet beauty of lovely flowers that may not get their full share of attention in the brilliance of daytime.

MARSH GARDENS

One of my friends recently bought a house in the country and came to me for some landscaping advice. Her idea of the perfect view from the new home's big side porch included a big, blooming flower garden. But her porch overlooked a low-lying area that was as soggy as an overdunked doughnut. "It's a *bog!*" she moaned. "What on earth can I do with a bog?"

"There's quite a lot you can do," I assured her. For gardeners with a spirit of adventure, a wet area offers a chance to try for some special effects. You can grow a wide range of attractive plants that would simply curl up their leaves at well-drained loam.

First, though, there's a question of identification to settle. My friend's wetland is really a marsh, not a bog. It has a small stream cutting through it. Areas with water flowing through them are marshes or swamps. Vegetation in a marsh is usually grassy, while a swamp is covered with trees or shrubs. And bogs differ from both. A bog, while it *may* be covered with either trees or herbaceous plants, is an area of near-stagnant, acidic water. Floating atop it is a mat of sedges, heaths, and sphagnum moss. The lack of oxygen in the still water prevents the decay of organic matter, and that allows peat to accumulate.

Each type of wetland suits different types of plants. Gardeners rarely have bogs on their land. In Britain, though, there are gardeners who actually build peat beds in an effort to duplicate natural bogs.

It's the more common marshy areas that really let a gardener in for some fun. In many regions, one of the first wildflowers to brighten winter-weary spirits is the bright yellow marsh marigold (*Caltha palustris*). This sunny member of the buttercup family needs lots of moisture all year round, so it's the perfect candidate for a marsh garden. A double form, 'Flore Pleno', has been developed but looks a bit too civilized to me; I think wetland plants should have an untamed air about them.

My family owns a little land in a portion of Vermont that has never known the interference of developers. We make a special effort each spring to drive up there when the marsh marigolds are in bloom. They're a startling sight, making a golden river that winds across a natural terrace in our hillside. The "river" is some twelve feet wide, so closely packed with marigolds that when a breeze blows, they billow and sink and billow again, glinting like rolling, sunstruck waves.

Moisture-loving irises will grow in a marsh. The beautiful blue flag (*Iris versicolor*) puts on its show in wet spots in early summer. Spiderwort (*Tradescantia*) is another early-summer bloomer. The native variety usually has blue flowers, but garden varieties come in anything from white to sky blue to reddish purple. They will grow in sun or light shade (and in medium to moist soil).

In summer, bright yellow ligularia and lysimachia will raise handsome spikes to the sun. Ligularias grow to three or four feet; lysimachia, commonly called yellow loosestrife, reaches a height of eighteen inches to three feet. Cardinal flower (*Lobelia cardinalis*), with its spire of bright red blooms, makes a stunning accent in the summer marsh garden.

For late summer, try bright yellow *Helenium autumnale* and the well-named turtlehead (*Chelone glabra*), with its pink and white blossoms that look like a group of snapping turtles dozing in the sun. Again, many of these plants, such as ligularia, lysimachia, and helenium, can also be grown away from the water's edge; but they'll be more luxuriant in moist soil.

When it comes to beautifying our homesites, we're lucky. Whether we have a desertlike section of sand or a soggy marsh, nature provides lovely plants that accept the conditions. With a bit of effort we can all look out on an inviting landscape.

MAKING A MEADOW

Years ago I was very impressed by a delightful wildflower garden in Dorset, Vermont. There were water-loving wild plants by and in a small pool; plants that like partial shade grew among trees in a little copse; and there was a spectacularly bright display of meadow flowers on a south-facing hillside. It was the first planned wildflower garden I'd ever seen.

Nowadays, more people are starting wildflower gardens; some with large acreages plant wildflower meadows. Several seed companies specializing in wildflower seeds have appeared, and their catalogs are quite clear about which plants thrive in what climates and locales.

Choices are broad. You can buy all annuals, all perennials, or a mix; you can plant a garden strictly for cut flowers, or a little meadow that changes its dress every few weeks. You can buy mixes for dry areas, shaded areas, or full sun. You can get vining wild plants, ground covers, flowers that grow from bulbs, and dozens of different kinds of ferns. But don't think it's as easy as shaking a can of seeds over your property and sitting back while California poppies burst into bloom and black-eyed Susans appear in a wink. It will pay for you to do a fair amount of study before you choose the varieties best for your meadow and invest in seeds (especially since you could be buying pounds of seeds for a field).

We've all seen daisies, black-eyed Susans, and Queen

Anne's lace growing along stony, dusty roadsides, so we know how tough wildflowers are. That should make them easy to grow, shouldn't it?

Well — yes. But if you plant wildflowers in rich garden soil, you may get more than you bargained for. Without accustomed competition from weeds, and with improved soil, some of the wildings may go crazy and try to take the place over. Don't fertilize at all if your soil is fair. If you want wildflowers for some really poor soil spots, fertilize only lightly.

Overpreparing the soil can cause problems too. At its headquarters in Mount Vernon, Virginia, the American Horticultural Society plowed six acres of land so they could plant a big wildflower meadow. They planted and waited. Thousands of little green shoots appeared — and every one turned out to be a pokeweed plant. The seeds had lain deep in the ground for almost a hundred years; those pokeweeds really went to town when deep plowing showed them some daylight. Shallow tilling is best.

Don't plant wild seeds too closely, as you probably won't be doing any thinning. Close plantings can mean that early flowers will grab all the space, leaving inadequate room for late bloomers.

Thorough weeding before planting is important. And since most of us don't know what wild plant seedlings look like, it helps to recognize "weedlings." We'd hate to pull out the daisies and leave the bindweed.

Wild plants aren't used to tender loving care; rather, they expect nature's erratic ways. However, if there is an unusually long dry spell, your wildflowers will appreciate extra water if you can provide it.

There is hardly an area of this country that doesn't have hundreds of lovely wild plants. Plants native to your own area are likely to be easy to care for — they are volunteer tenants who liked the place so much they stayed for years.

———◦ 4 ◦———

Repotting House Plants

When we're in the throes of a late-February snowstorm, it's hard to believe that the days have been getting longer ever since the winter solstice in December. That means just one thing — spring is on its way.

Most of us appreciate the longer hours of daylight, and we're not the only ones. House plants may not get psychologically depressed because the days are short and often gloomy, but they sure do get physically depressed. Plants need light to grow, and they react to the shorter, darker days of winter by slowing their growth. This means that during winter most house plants have a reduced need for water and fertilizer, unless you're supplementing natural light with artificial light. It also means that when days begin to lengthen, you'll probably see a spurt of growth as plants switch into high gear again.

Like children whose last year's clothes are inevitably too short and too tight, your house plants may find their quarters are getting overcrowded. An ideal time to repot them is late winter or early spring, when they're beginning that growth spurt. Besides, if you wait until late March and April, your attention is already focused on the young seedlings you're raising for the outdoor garden.

Not every house plant needs repotting every year. Some of the fast growers, like asparagus ferns, are bursting their buttons; others, like clivias, bloom best when somewhat pot-bound. They're usually content in the same pot for three or four years.

You may wonder why we don't just put all our plants in big pots and let them grow to fit. It's not a good practice, for if there is too great a volume of soil in relation to the number of plant roots, the roots won't be able to take up water from the soil at the proper rate. The soil will stay wet too long, and the roots will rot. The general rule when moving a plant to a larger pot is to use one that's an inch larger in diameter than the pot it grew in previously; if it's a big plant, allow two inches.

To see whether it's time to repot, slide the plant part way out of its pot and take a look at the root system. If you water a plant at night, it's easier to get it out of the pot in the morning. Slide your hand over the top of the pot, holding the plant stem with two fingers, carefully tip the pot over, and tap the edge sharply against a kitchen counter edge. If roots have grown to the outer surface of the soil ball, it's time to repot. If they're growing in circles around the soil ball, it's *really* time to repot.

Quite large plants and pots are harder to handle, so yell for help. Rap the top of the pot with a padded mallet to help loosen the soil ball; then have your helper get two hands under the plant as you slide it out. You can see the root ball when the plant's about halfway out.

To start the plant in its new home, very gently unwind some of the root ball to give it the idea that it will soon have plenty of room to stretch. Set the plant into the new pot at its accustomed depth. Pack the new soil in well around the old root ball to eliminate air pockets. Then water thoroughly.

Put your repotted plants where they, and you, can enjoy the brightening sun and the slowly but surely lengthening days with their promise of summer.

∘ 5 ∘

Spring-Flowering Trees

SHADBLOW

The first robin, who usually struts about the lawn in late February in the mistaken conviction he's the harbinger of spring, doesn't fool me for a minute. Neither does the more modest but overoptimistic first crocus. I've seen both of them shivering in a snowstorm.

Like many gardeners, I watch for the flowering of the tree we call shad or shadblow (after the fact that its bloom coincides with the spawning runs of the shad up Eastern rivers). The delicate, glowing white flowers of the shad are a sure sign that the earth is ready for some garden planting.

Shad, which belongs to the genus *Amelanchier*, is widely known as serviceberry, also as Juneberry, sarvis, May cherry, sugar plum, sugar pear, wild pear, and half a dozen other things, depending on where it grows. "Serviceberry" is a very apt name for the tree, because service is what it provides.

Adapted to many climates and soils, self-pollinating, thickly veiled in lovely blossoms at a time when most other trees are just waking up, serviceberry needs almost no care and provides reddish-purple fruits that are good in many cooked dishes.

Different species have different growth habits; some are bushlike, others are tall trees. The berries are small, so they don't make a mess on the ground.

With two exceptions, the *Amelanchiers* are native to this country. The fruits have been part of the American diet for many years. Native Americans and early colonial settlers mixed serviceberries with buffalo meat and fat to make pemmican, which sustained travelers as they journeyed. *A. alnifolia* is called saskatoon; the Indian name of the fruit was mis-sask-qua-too-min. The Canadian city of Saskatoon acquired its name because of the abundance of these trees nearby. One cultivar of the saskatoon, 'Altaglow', makes a beautiful ornamental. It has a narrow habit, grows up to twenty feet tall, and has foliage that changes in fall to rich shades of purple, red, and yellow. Its fruits, unlike most serviceberries, are cream-colored.

Another serviceberry recommended as an edible ornamental is *A. grandiflora*, or apple serviceberry, so called because of the large size of its pure white blossoms. It too changes in fall, when leaves become purple or yellow.

Serviceberry trees are a good choice for home landscapes. Some tend to grow quite tall, but it's easy to keep the tops pruned back and the fruits within easy reach. In winter, the tree bark is lovely, striped grey with a hint of pink, and velvety smooth. The only drawback is that most species are prone to insect problems.

The Allegheny serviceberry (*A. laevis*) produces small

purplish fruits that have a faintly almond flavor. They can be eaten right from the tree, but most people cook them. Their juice is excellent, especially mixed with apple or strawberry juice for jelly or jam. You don't need special recipes to use serviceberries in baked goods; just substitute them in your favorite blueberry recipes.

DOGWOOD

I miss my pretty Pennsylvania dogwood. I used to love eating my lunch on the back porch and admiring its clouds of white bloom. I had to give it up when I moved. That's the trouble — when gardeners move we can't bring along our gardens, though we might be able to pack a few roots or cuttings from favorite plants. We have to start our fruit or ornamental shrubs and trees all over again in the new place.

After I married and moved to Vermont, I realized there was little point in planting a dogwood; it's too cold here for the lovely little trees. Ah, well — most gardeners who move to different climate zones have to change what they plant; many things will flower or fruit well only in particular zones.

I'm lucky enough to live in the Champlain Valley, where the miniclimate (USDA Zone 5) is fairly warm because of the influence of the huge lake, so I can plant some less-hardy shrubs or trees successfully. In fact, flowering dogwood (*Cornus florida*) will survive here, because the trees are comparatively hardy. But their buds rarely get a chance to open. The buds are likely to be killed three winters out of five, and after all, they're what I want the tree for.

I shouldn't talk casually about dogwood "flowers," of course. The pretty white or pink petals, with their indentations as if they'd been hand punched around the edges, are really bracts, or modified leaves. But since everyone calls them flowers, I do the same, and we all know what we're talking about. Flowering dogwood puts on a show in autumn, too, when the leaves turn a lovely red-orange. The glossy red berries ripen in fall and attract birds.

Japanese dogwood (*C. kousa*) is the Asiatic counterpart of our native dogwood. It's supposedly hardy to Zone 5, though I haven't had the nerve to try it in my own back yard. Perhaps the best advantage of planting Japanese dogwood is that it's not susceptible to a serious fungus disease called dogwood anthracnose, which affects dogwoods in southern New England and the mid-Atlantic states.

If your winters are fairly mild, dogwoods with their lovely bloom and horizontal branching habit are an excellent choice for the yard, and they don't need as much space as many landscape trees. Northern gardeners can often succeed with a cousin of flowering dogwood, the pagoda dogwood (*C. alternifolia*). It hasn't the flower power of the flowering dogwood I miss so much, but it's still a lovely tree. It has the same attractive horizontal branches, and its blossoms are yellow-white and fragrant, though not showy. The fruits are bluish black and ripen in late summer. The pagoda dogwood looks best in an informal country setting.

Some day I hope to see the Pacific dogwood (*C. nuttallii*) in bloom. Many consider it our finest native flowering tree. It thrives only in the mild, moist climate of the Pacific Northwest. Its bracts are huge, four or five inches across, each with six petals instead of the four we're accustomed to on eastern dogwoods. These trees can grow to seventy-five or even one hundred feet tall, and have scarlet and yellow fall foliage. How magnificent those giants must look.

While dogwoods are fine ornamentals, they're also useful. Persons who can weave (and don't I wish I could) appreciate dogwoods for utilitarian reasons. Virtually all the shuttles on looms are made from the wood of dogwoods. The wood is quite dense in texture, so shuttles made of it are smooth and durable, causing very little wear on the thread. The same qualities make dogwood useful for golf club heads, mallet heads, and wooden knitting needles. In fact, the name dogwood is supposed to have come from the old word "dag," which meant a skewer used to hold meat for cooking.

CRABAPPLES

One of my favorite childhood streets was a pleasant enough thoroughfare most of the year, though cars often drove too fast on it. It was a wide avenue with a broad, tree-filled median dividing the lanes of traffic. In May traffic slowed sharply because the trees' flowers burst open — the effect was breathtaking.

These were crabapples, some of the most popular small flowering trees and with good reason. They're hardy; they're easy to grow; they come in enough shapes and sizes to fit just about any landscape; and their flowers, as you see, promote traffic safety.

They weren't always so popular. Crabapples have been around for a long time, but weren't used as ornamentals until the middle of this century. Before that, they were valued mainly for their fruits. The small apples are too sour to eat out of hand, but for centuries have been used to make delicious amber-colored jelly. Nowadays, gardeners are often more interested in the beauty of the fruits. Ranging in color from red to yellow, and in size from a pea to a plum, crabapple fruits add interest to the landscape in late summer and fall; on some varieties, they even remain on the tree through most of the winter.

Still, it's the springtime flowers that make many gardeners include at least one crabapple in the landscape. Whether pure white, delicate pink, or deep, rosy red, the blooms are often fragrant. Some varieties have single flowers; many are semidouble. That means they have more petals than the usual flower, but not so many that they abandon most of their stamens and pistils, as many true double blooms do. Showy double-flowered varieties keep their flowers on the tree longest, but fruiting is likely to be sparse.

Crabapples need good drainage and a sunny spot, but they're not fussy about soil. You don't need to prune a crabapple, except to remove suckers from the tree's base. Like apples grown for fruit, crabapples are usually grafted; suckers arising from the base will have the characteristics of the rootstock rather than those of the grafted top of the tree.

A problem many gardeners face with crabapples is disease. Like their larger-fruited cousins, crabs are prone to infections of fire blight, cedar apple rust, and apple scab. Unfortunately, some of the most beautiful varieties, such as 'Hopa', 'Almey', and 'Eleyi', are very susceptible to disease, particulary apple scab.

You'll still find these varieties commonly offered for sale, but for those who prefer not to worry about sprays, there are other beautiful choices, less likely to have problems. 'Adams', for example, has single, deep pink flowers, red fruits, and a rounded growth habit reaching about twenty feet at maturity; it is very disease resistant. 'Katherine' is another usually trouble-free variety, with double flowers that start pink and fade to white, followed by yellow fruits. Other disease-resistant crabs include 'Dolgo', 'David', and 'Mary Potter'. Sometimes you'll run across disagreements about crabapples; some growers may declare that a certain variety is free of most pest and disease problems, while others say it isn't. The differences arise, no doubt, because plants face different conditions in different parts of the country. My advice is to talk to local gardeners and nurseries to learn what crabapple varieties have done best in your area.

My city planted scores of these delightful trees along the streets and at shopping centers. They don't get much tender loving care, and they still show no resentment. They're gorgeous in their spring bloom, and their fruits are attractive on the trees all fall.

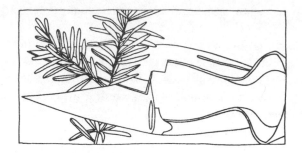

∘ 6 ∘

Landscaping
at the Pages·

Every spring I wonder, is ours the only family where the male and female views of neatness vary 180 degrees? To the men in my family, any house is neatest and most attractive when practically empty. Shelves cleared, desk tops barren, chairs and tables pushed back to the walls, acres of bare carpet over as much of the floor as possible. The closer to an army barracks the better: utter neatness is utter blankness is beauty.

Not to the females in my family. To us, bare, clean walls, empty desks, deserted shelves are boring, not beautiful. (I'll admit there are times, when I see the chaos one busy week can produce, I feel a twinge of sympathy for the male viewpoint.)

The same sex-linked reaction occurs with our outdoor landscape. Acres of empty lawn, perhaps edged by a few low, carefully cropped bushes, are the male preference. The eager-beaver neatening urge usually strikes on the first warm spring day, when the blanketing snow is gone and the winter-bedraggled growth is visible. My husband will look out at the straggly wild raspberries, volunteer maples, and skinny shadblow trees. "Next thing you know, we won't be able to see the view at all," he'll mutter as he grabs the saw and the loppers.

"Please, don't cut down all the wild plants," I'll shout after him. "They'll be beautiful in a few weeks!"

It took a few years for my daughters and me to realize what we were up against. The controversy came to a head when the men removed our huge, ancient apple tree because it never produced any fruit, though it did provide one breathtaking week each spring, when rich white blooms hung like a tapestry against the background of indigo lake and sapphire sky.

Since then it's been something of a pitched battle between overbarren and overbedecked, but we've worked out compromises. For one thing, we have learned how to control trees and shrubs better.

There's a difference between pruning and shearing. Bushes or trees that are sheared are cut to some arbitrary form determined in advance by the gardener. The bushes that must stay low, like those under windows, we shear in this heartless way, with army-style crewcuts. But such formality isn't appropriate for all our shrubs, even though we don't want them sprawling. To keep a shrub at a particular size without altering its natural growth habit, we prune individual branches back to a side branch or bud lower down on the branch. That way we maintain neatness without creating an artificial appearance.

As for when to prune shrubs, there's a handy rule of thumb. If a shrub blooms in spring, prune right after it's through flowering. If you wait too long, you'll be cutting off the flower buds for next year. If a shrub blooms in summer, prune in early spring, as that shrub sets its flower buds on new wood in the current season.

With evergreens, we give the first pruning after the initial flush of lime-green growth in early summer. We prune later only if they get too high or begin to look ragged.

Our compromise is working, at least outdoors. No spots are barren, but the place doesn't look like the Sleeping Beauty's protective forest, either.

—○ 7 ○—

Lessons in Buying and Planting Trees

A few years ago my husband and I went to the local nursery in search of a small flowering tree for one corner of our house. When we got to the nursery to make our selection, we found trees with bare roots, trees in plastic pots, trees in big tubs, and trees with burlap wrapped around their roots. There were a few we liked but we couldn't tell which ones were the healthiest. We chose one in a container because it seemed best suited for our house. Our tree survived the first year and now is a permanent member of our landscape. But we might not have been so lucky.

Potted trees can be "container grown," having been in their pots since they were seedlings; or they can be field-grown plants that have been dug up and put into pots for display purposes. The container-grown plants have had time to develop good, compact root systems, which makes them easy to transplant almost any time. Because of the care they've had, these tend to be the most expensive choices.

Dug and potted plants are a different story. When they're in their dormant stage, these have about the same survival rate as bare-root plants, which is usually pretty good. But if a dug and potted plant begins to leaf out before you get it into the ground, you may be in trouble. The tree probably hasn't had time to get established in the pot and its root ball may fall apart the moment you place it in the hole. You can tell whether your tree is container grown or "containerized" by giving it a gentle tug. The container-grown tree will resist your tug and stay firmly in its pot.

You may also find bare-root plants at the nursery. This is the way most trees arrive if you order through a catalog. The roots are usually protected by moist packing material. These trees were dug during the dormant season and they should be planted while they're still dormant. They're not as expensive as container-grown or burlap-wrapped trees, because it costs much less to ship them. If you ever happen to get any bare-root stock that seems to be breaking dormancy and putting out leaves, get it into the ground as fast as possible. Though there is some food stored in the roots, when a plant starts to grow it needs soil for water and nutrients.

The burlap-wrapped trees, commonly referred to as "B and B" for "balled and burlapped," have been dug from the field. The balls of roots, with the soil still attached, are dug up and wrapped in burlap. Such plants will cost more than bare-root trees, because of the labor involved. During the growing season, these are excellent choices. Evergreens are often sold this way.

Getting the tree home after you've selected it is another problem. We recently bought a pickup truck that we use to carry our plants back from the nursery, but for years we had to rely on the nursery to deliver our purchases. A friend of mine told me of an experience that made me realize how lucky we are to have a truck.

She had bought a lovely maple tree, a good-sized one, at a nursery, and it cost two hundred dollars. At that price, she wanted to be sure it was cared for during delivery, so she paid the nursery an extra twenty-five dollars to bring it to her house.

She had personally selected the maple tree; it was balled and burlapped and had not leafed out, so she felt sure she could get it into the ground before its spring revival. She and her husband dug a good, roomy hole and awaited delivery.

The tree came eight days later. Meanwhile, New England had produced one of its sudden early-spring warm spells. The delivery truck pulled up on a sunny day with their tree lying in back. My friends were horrified to see the tree's leafy top waving in the breeze; they knew that a tree in leaf dries out very rapidly in the wind generated by a moving vehicle. The tree's top should have been covered with a tarp to protect it during the move.

When they approached the pickup truck, they saw that the tree had just been shoved in, its trunk resting against the side of the truck bed. There was no padding, so some of the tender bark had been rubbed away during the journey. Any bark wound can serve as an entry for disease-causing fungi.

The last straw was when the deliveryman, who was a trucker, not a plantsman, dropped the tree off the back of the truck with a thud, right onto its large, wrapped root ball, a surefire way to break or crack roots within the ball.

My friend said they planted the tree carefully and watered it deeply and regularly, hoping it could recover. But by the next spring it had died. Luckily she had bought her tree at a local nursery that guaranteed its products, so she was given a replacement. This time she and her husband made arrangements to pick up the tree themselves. It's always a good idea to get a written quality guarantee from the nursery where you purchase your trees.

Of course, the long-term health of a tree depends on more than just the condition in which it arrives at your house. You've got to give it the right conditions to grow in. It's usually best to prepare the hole in the fall for planting a tree the following spring.

Too many of us spoil our new trees. In the traditional tree-planting method, we take a spade, dig a big slick hole, much larger than the young tree roots seem to require. Then we put in a rich mixture of compost, soil, blood meal, rotted manure, and anything else we think would make a good organic treat for the tree. And as the tree goes into the hole, we make sure it gets ample water. The watering is fine, but let's look back at where we started.

All that rich food was tucked into a hole that has been dug with a spade and has slick, firm sides. That can make a tree become just as pot-bound as a potted plant indoors. The young tree roots, growing joyously in their fast-food environment, suddenly hit the walls of the hole. Like plant roots in a flowerpot, they aren't going to work hard to get through that solid wall. Sometimes you can actually pull mature trees out of the ground, their roots in a tangled, pot-bound mess.

It's OK to dig with a spade — it would take forever any other way — but after making the hole nice and roomy, you should take a digging fork and break up its bottom and sides. The cracking and breaking will make it easier for the tree roots to spread into the surrounding area.

As you dig, separate the soil from the sod and weeds. Put perennial weeds in a pile to burn. Other weeds and the sod should go into the compost pile. Mix the soil you've saved with small amounts of mineral fertilizers. Rock phosphate, superphosphate, bone meal, oyster shell, and wood ash are

all good mineral sources. Incorporate the phosphate and pot-
ash deep down into the hole, because they don't leach into
the soil more than a few inches and you want to make sure
they'll be available to all the roots.

Finally, cover the refilled hole with mulch and leave it
throughout the skiing and snow-shoveling season.

In spring, when you're ready to plant, your approach depends on whether you have an unusually wet environment
or not.

In most situations, once the tree is in and the backfilling
is almost completed, you can mix into the top layer of soil
some of the goodies you've gathered to nurture your new
tree — compost, rotted manure, leaf mold. Water the tree
well, complete the backfilling, and build a low dike or sau-
cer of soil around the rim of the planting hole to retain
water.

If you have extremely wet springs, though, you'll need to
take precautions against crown rot. Mound up the soil in
the planting hole about a foot above the surrounding surface. The mound will settle, but the crown of the root system will still be high enough for good drainage. As you heap
up the mound you can enrich the soil with all those organic
additions. Water, then mulch with hay or leaves so the
mound won't dry out too quickly.

With this kind of well-controlled care, your young trees
should have long and healthy lives.

—— ∘ 8 ∘ ——

Feeding the Good Earth

COMPOST

Composting plant leftovers not only helps feed tomorrow's new plants but fits the "waste not, want not" outlook of many of us who garden. There are books and articles by the score on what compost is, how to start a pile, what the optimum size is, and how to achieve the best ratios of ingredients.

Some of the literature provides such exacting carbon-to-nitrogen ratio recommendations, you'd need a chemistry lab to work them out. Usually all you need to remember is that you want a lot more carbon than you do nitrogen, but you must have some nitrogen to speed fermentation. Dried plant materials, from autumn leaves to straw and hay, are high in carbon; fresh ones are high in nitrogen.

Knowing no way to measure the nitrogen in two armfuls of grass clippings, or the carbon in a basket of dry leaves, I try to make sure I have ample amounts of both carbon and nitrogen. I also add some soil so that its microorganisms can get to work on decaying my pile. It's not a highly scientific formula, but Nature has used it for years and seems to be doing OK.

In terms of speed, however, most gardeners want to go Nature one better. She's efficient enough for forest work and for the broad spectrum of green growth around the globe. But as the old Yankee said when told the Alaskan glacier he stood on was moving, "She's slow, though, Earl, ain't she? Mighty slow."

The kind of compost pile you have depends in part on the space you have. We're lucky — at my house we have ample room for four four- by five-foot rectangular bins for composting. Each is about three and a half feet high. To mix and aerate the slowly disintegrating material we move it from one section to the next, stirring and turning it as we go. Compost in the final bin has thus been through three moves.

The bins are made of ancient railroad ties that may soon have to be replaced with concrete blocks. The blocks, set so their holes admit air into the pile, work well, though they're a bit heavy to handle. Many people use wire cages, or buy compost bins that provide an easy way to get the completed mixture out at the bottom.

We start our compost heap by laying some branches from our tree prunings at the bottom of each bin, to be sure air can circulate. We top the branches with various compost materials. It's always a boost if you can get some animal manure into the pile. We use horse manure because it's readily available, but first we give it time to break down completely. If we don't, we'll end up planting weed seeds when we spread the compost; horses' digestions don't destroy them. We also toss into the pile kitchen garbage, prunings, plant thinnings (so long as the plants were healthy), weed tops before they go to seed, autumn leaves — just about anything organic and rottable.

Most gardeners don't put in animal scraps or bones from the table, because they can attract foraging critters. We're not perfect about this, so occasionally I'll turn up the odd chicken drumstick when I'm weeding around the lettuce or tomatoes. I've no idea how long bones take to compost completely, but after a year in the compost pile, any bones we've carelessly dumped in with the garbage are white and light as a feather. I suspect most of their compostable goodies have already been delivered.

How fast your compost works depends partly on you and partly on the warmth of the weather. If you turn the pile regularly and frequently — say every week — and make sure it's always moist but not soggy, and if the weather stays warm, you may get usable compost in six weeks. If you just throw stuff on the pile and do nothing, you'll still get compost but it will probably take two years. Our own approach to compost is midway between these fast and slow extremes. We stir ours from time to time when we think of it, and move it from bin to bin every three months. With that loose system, it takes a year to get compost. It's beautiful stuff, though — rich, dark, sweet smelling, and full of the fattest earthworms you ever saw.

MANURE

Every true gardener feels that manure magically and dramatically improves garden soil, but most of us are unsure about what kinds to use and how much. And more than a few of us are timid about adding fresh manure because it could bring with it a host of weed seeds, fungi, undesirable microoganisms, or other unwanted additions.

Many garden books and magazines offer charts giving a rough idea of how much nitrogen, phosphorus, and potassium there are in various kinds of manure, from elephant and giraffe to chicken and bat, but such charts aren't one hundred percent accurate. Much depends on the age and size of the animal, the type of feed it's had, how the manure's been stored and for how long, and other factors.

You don't need to be that accurate — besides, how many of us have easy access to giraffe manure? Because manure also conditions and makes soil more friable, it is worth using whether or not it's high in the three major plant nutrients. All manure contains *some* of the major plant nutrients, as well as trace minerals, and organic matter to keep essential soil organisms thriving.

The ideal is to be able to add manure to the garden beds every year, say an inch or so over the entire area. Poultry, horse, and cattle manures are common and all are good. Other good manures come from pigs, goats (a mild-smelling dung, which makes it good for use near the house), rabbits, sheep, and bats. The best way to get bat guano, which is also mild smelling, is to buy it packaged. Don't try gathering it yourself from caves, even if you live conveniently near some. Old droppings contain a fungus that causes respiratory disease; besides, amateur collectors of guano can threaten endangered bat species. Never use cat or dog dung in the garden; both often contain disease organisms.

Some gardeners get sewage sludge from the hometown sewage treatment plant for use on flower gardens and lawns. This can be an excellent soil conditioner and plant feeder, but it may be contaminated by heavy metals that are very dangerous to human health. If your city sells its sludge as compost or soil conditioner, inquire whether it is regularly tested for possible heavy metal contamination. If it isn't, don't use it. And regardless of what the city says, never use sewage sludge on your food garden. You don't want to put your family's health at risk.

In adding dung to the garden, sometimes I think we worry too much about timing. It's true that ammonia in manure can burn plant roots; but cattle and pig manures have a high water content and so are considered "cool." If you mix them thoroughly with the soil around your plants, making sure they don't touch the plants themselves, they're not likely to do damage. Or you can just age these manures for two to five weeks before using them in the garden. Horse manure is another story. It's likely to be full of weed seeds, so if you add it when it's even moderately fresh you're likely to be planting weeds all over the pea patch. Always compost horse manure before using.

The so-called "hot" manures are great for turning a cold frame into a hotbed. Put down an eight-inch layer of fresh chicken, goat, sheep, horse, or rabbit dung and cover it with six inches of topsoil. These manures are so hot you should wait about a week before planting anything in the hotbed.

So, though others are surprised to hear it on your tongue — you're a gardener. Why not praise your favorite dung?

GREEN MANURES

Two acquaintances cornered me recently at a shopping mall. They were indignant. "You keep telling us on the radio to add all these organic materials to our gardens," they said in essence, "but where do we get them? Where we live, manure and seaweed and autumn leaves in any quantity are almost as scarce as uranium. What are we supposed to do?"

I sympathized. For some folks, it can take so much time

to round up rich organic materials for the soil, there's hardly enough time left to plant anything.

"Grow your own," I suggested to my friends.

"What?" said they.

"You can, you know," I assured them. The best answer to this fairly common problem is to raise some legumes (like peas, beans, or clover) or grasses (like rye or buckwheat), then till them under to improve the soil. Their roots mine the soil, opening it to better movement of air and water. Some deep-rooted ones pull up minerals from the subsoil that your plants can use. And legumes have the added bonus of adding nitrogen to the soil. These cover crops, also called green manures, add real wealth to the garden.

Legumes are a marvel in the horticultural world. While they grow they "fix" nitrogen from the air spaces in the soil. That means that certain types of bacteria that live in the legume roots take nitrogen from the air and change it into a form that plants can take up and use. When you till the legumes under, you add nitrogen to your garden and improve its tilth. Be warned that among the legumes, alfalfa is a perennial, and without special planning and care, you may end up with a weed problem. I'd recommend against alfalfa for beginners.

We always use our peas as a cover crop, because we can eat the crop and use it for green manure too. We return the empty pea pods to the garden and till them in, along with all the pea vines; then the soil is rich enough to support other plantings.

I think tillers are the key to successful cover cropping. Even in small gardens, digging in green manures by hand is difficult. It's really worth borrowing a small tiller or paying someone to turn under your crop to get the job done efficiently. Tillers are also good because they chop up the plants as they turn them under; the chopping speeds the plants' decomposition and release of nutrients. This system is called power composting and requires a rear-end tiller, which has the weight and strength to do the chop-and-bury job.

For those who don't have tillers, cover cropping sounds tedious. But perhaps it need not be. Start planting your annual ryegrass, winter rye, or buckwheat while other crops are still waiting to be picked. Winter or annual rye among the bean rows won't hurt a thing. Your current crops will all be harvested before the cover crop makes it to third grade.

That way, you don't have the entire garden to plant all at once. If you use raised beds, you can do the same thing; or you can put a cover crop in as a succession crop. After the melons or tomatoes have been harvested, put in the winter cover crop. It can start growing while your cold-hardy vegetables continue to laugh at light frosts.

Here's another formula for crop rotation that includes a green manure. In the North we work out a regular system to keep our garden soil rich all the time. We plant peas in early spring and till them in in late June. Then we set out our cabbage or broccoli transplants. When their harvest is over, we add their chopped remains to the soil (assuming they're not diseased) and broadcast annual rye seed. Leave it in the garden over the winter, adding some 10-10-10 fertilizer and lime, if needed, to assure quick growth. By early spring, the rye crop will have died. Till it in and leave it a few weeks to decompose, then plant peas again.

Another tip for gardeners without tillers is to mow down the tops of the cover crop and put them on the compost pile; you'll return those to the garden later. It's much easier to turn under the shorn crop that's still in the field.

Some gardeners try to prepare the rotation crop for tilling by blanketing it with black plastic. A few weeks without light should kill the plants and all the weeds. Of course, depending on your garden size, you may need a lot of plastic.

And you must be very careful to fasten the plastic's edges down securely or shiny black clouds may soon decorate every tree or utility wire in the neighborhood.

Timing's important with crops that form seeds, as do the grasses. You don't want them to come up as weeds in your garden the next year. Avoid the problem by planting cover crops in fall. They'll have a long enough season to get started, but winter will arrive before the plants even consider forming seeds.

To a real gardener, cover cropping becomes a habit. Once you've become used to it, you will itch to cover-crop every vacant field you see.

SUPPLEMENTAL FEEDINGS

Can you remember, each week during the summer, which of your plants are ready for their regular doses of fertilizer? I never can; I always end up checking my trusty gardening book, which I keep right inside the kitchen door.

"Side-dressing," as it's called, can give your plants a real boost just when they need it. Of course I know the peas and beans don't need side-dressing at all, they're legumes and can fix their own nitrogen. Cabbage and cauliflower also manage without side-dressing, bless their hearts, especially in our compost-rich soil.

With all the vining crops there's a rule of thumb that helps: side-dress them when the vines begin to run, and again when the blossoms appear. I just wish the squashes and melons and cukes would all do those things at the same time, but of course that's too much to ask.

We should side-dress beets raised for greens just two weeks after the leaves first appear. Uh-oh, I didn't do that this year. At any rate, those I want to grow into sizable beets

I will simply encourage with a hearty meal of manure-rich compost scratched in along the rows.

Broccoli and Brussels sprouts like to be side-dressed about three weeks after they're transplanted. The sprouts like another feed when they start appearing in their cozy nooks along the stalk, and I won't forget that, because we love having loads of sprouts into late fall.

Carrots should be side-dressed three weeks after the plants are well established, which to me means when the tops lose that featherish look and start to grow their sturdier stems. Corn, of course, is always hungry. We side-dress corn three times: three weeks after planting, again when plants are eight inches high, and the third time when they start to tassel out.

We've never side-dressed our potatoes and always get a good crop; but my book says they should get a feed when the plants bloom, so we'll do that this year, especially as we've planted fewer than usual.

As for tomatoes, you'd think I'd remember after growing them for so many years. They should be side-dressed two to three weeks after transplanting, and again when there are plenty of green tomatoes appearing, but still none ready for harvest. Usually I get so excited watching for the first tomato to ripen — sometimes it's well into August before that happens — I forget about that side-dressing. Now I draw a red tomato at the beginning of our August calendar as a reminder.

We side-dress with manure-rich compost, and sometimes also use foliar feeds. For foliar feeding we like fish emulsion and liquid kelp, which we dissolve right in the watering can to save time and work. We don't worry much about the amounts per plant when we use feeds like this. However, with chemical fertilizers it's important to be a bit cautious. You can use dry fertilizer and work it into the soil with your hands, in a little circle around each plant — about a tablespoonful of 5-10-10 for each smaller plant, or two table-spoons for big ones like Brussels sprouts or tomatoes. If it's easier, just sprinkle the fertilizer along the row of plants and scratch it in a bit with one of those pronged weeders or a rake. Or use liquid houseplant fertilizer.

Overdoing any fertilizer can encourage fertilizer salts to build up in the soil. The risk is greater with the commercial products because they're more concentrated.

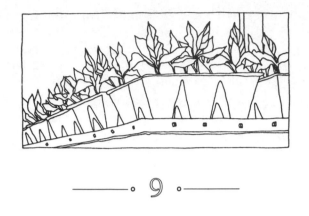

—— ◦ 9 ◦ ——

Secrets to
Buying Transplants

In Africa, many nurseries throw away bedding plants that burst into bloom before they're sold. No one will buy them, because everyone knows that transplants are stronger and better if they're not trying to support flowers.

Yet in the United States, people seem to be afraid that if they buy a flowering plant with no flowers showing, it may never produce any; or maybe they don't trust the color until they see it. We shouldn't have such suspicious natures.

When you buy petunias, don't grab the flats full of plants covered with soft, rippling flowers. Take plants that have no flowers at all or very few, but that are well-branched, green, and healthy looking. They'll transplant with less shock and go on to blossom much better than their precocious sister plants sporting blossoms on the sale table.

Sometimes you have no choice. You didn't get around to

visiting the nursery until late. All the petunias are blooming. Buy some. When you get home, plant them and grimly
pinch off every single bloom, to encourage the plant to create new branches.

Containers are another clue to healthy bedding plants.
Cell packs, in which each plant has its own small square,
are best, because the roots of the plants can't tangle with
each other. Often there are less expensive plants in groups
of six or eight all growing in one container. These "one big
happy family" types are trickier to transplant; you end up
lopping off some of the roots.

Don't (as I have done in the past but promise never to do
again) extricate a few plants with your kitchen fork, then
try to untangle the roots. They're far worse than that web
of hangers in your coat closet, believe me. At this point you
can only get the plants apart by tearing some of the roots.

Instead, take action a week before you intend to transplant. Block out each individual plant. With a sharp knife,
cut a square of soil around each plant. After cutting through
the soil to the bottom, wiggle your knife from side to side
just a bit to be sure the plant is fully separated. Cutting with
a knife prunes the roots but doesn't tear them, and the pruning encourages new root growth.

Incidentally, my husband and I have often used peat pots
to start our own transplants. With peat pots you plant pot
and all and thus never disturb those tender, reaching roots.
We've found that even these aren't perfect, though. Sometimes the roots reach the wall of the pot and can't break
through. Perhaps this happens because we use a soilless
mix; it dries so fast the pot walls never get enough moisture
to soften them.

Do two things when you set out transplants in peat pots.
First, tear off the upper lip of the pot so it can't act like a
wick and draw moisture away from the plant. Next, tear the
pot walls a bit as you set it in the planting hole. That way

the reaching plant roots will never come to a stop — or even a yield — sign.

Besides flowers and containers, the third thing to consider when buying transplants is size. The bigger they are, the harder they fall. That's not just true of pine trees and politicos, it's true of bedding plants. Don't buy big; buy small.

Last summer, we made the mistake of waiting far too long to buy our Brussels sprouts. All the ones in the nursery had grown too much and were root-bound in their small pots. We knew that would mean a real setback at transplant time, but we gave them a try. We soon learned another lesson. (We learn quite a few every year in the garden.) Some of those plants, while they stayed green and fairly healthy looking, just never did anything. We gave them full benefits of water and nutrients all summer, but most never signed up for employment. About October 1, a few woke up and apparently realized they were supposed to be producing Brussels sprouts. They formed some of the tiniest sprouts you ever saw. The rest remained cases of retarded development, eternally in their early teens.

This summer, we'll either start our own brassica plants, or buy young ones; never again will we bother to set out any that have been stressed by too long a period of incarceration. We don't need any irresponsible hangers-on in the garden.

There's another good reason to buy fresh, young plants. The babies realize their job is to grow big and strong before they set fruit; then they'll be able to produce a great big family. Those that have flowered or begun to fruit before you buy them may produce, all right, but they'll spend all their energy on fruiting, rather than on growing bigger so they can support more and larger fruits.

Researchers at Cornell University did a study on this subject. They found that pepper plants that had no buds when set out produced not only greater yields, but actually earlier yields, than transplants with flowers or developing fruit.

In Kansas, pepper trials showed that eight-week-old transplants produced earlier and larger fruit than eleven-week-old transplants. However, the Kansas researchers learned something else that may be helpful if you must buy pepper plants with flowers and/or fruits. When growers removed all buds, flowers, small fruits, and growing tips from the plants two or three weeks before transplanting them, they got more early, table-ready peppers.

Two more brief tips: first, when buying bedding plants, ask the salesperson to show you the plant roots, or check them yourself. Carefully slide the transplants out of the pack for a moment. If the roots aren't white, don't buy the plant; it may end up with root rot. And lastly, if you find plants with tangled root balls, don't set them in the ground like that. Ever so gently massage the little mass of soil and roots between your hands first; that will encourage roots to grow outward.

If all goes well, and you don't have an extra late frost, the young flowers and vegetables will perk up after a day or two in the soil. By midsummer you should have bountiful supplies of both beautiful flowers and fresh vegetables.

─── ∘ 10 ∘ ───

Dressing Up the House

PORCH PLANTS

At the turn of the century, most houses in this country had porches. The porch was the social center of the home during warm weather, the place where people sat at the end of a hot day to relax and chat with passing neighbors. It was a place to curl up with a good book on a lazy summer afternoon, a place for the kids to play when the weather turned rainy. After World War II, the front porch disappeared, replaced by a deck in the back yard or an air-conditioned room in the house. Today, as people are rediscovering the joys of porch-sitting, the front porch is making something of a comeback.

For me, the epitome of porches was the one that went around three sides of the big Victorian summer house my family rented in a small Pennsylvania town. The house stood on a street lined on both sides with towering elms whose branches interlaced, creating a leafy tunnel. From the broad front porch you could see all that went on, up and down the street. You could wave to neighbors sitting on *their* front porches, and exchange hellos with passersby. At the end of the side porch was that indispensable item for porch-sitting, a glider. Climbing the trellis behind it, making an almost solid green backdrop, was one of the favorite vines of that era, Dutchman's pipe (*Aristolochia durior*).

For me, a porch is not complete without a vine curling up a post or twining along a railing. A festoon of greenery links house and porch to the garden. It provides privacy, delicious scents, and the soporific sound of rustling leaves. Dutchman's pipe has heart-shaped leaves that may be up to a foot long, and its stems can reach thirty feet or longer. It gets its name from the small flowers that are usually hidden by the leaves; they look like miniature meerschaum pipes. Because the overlapping leaves stay flat against a trellis, they're great for screening.

In a smaller, modern house you may find a delicate-textured vine more fitting. There are lots of choices. If it's flowers you're after, there are few sights as beautiful as a clematis in full bloom. Like Dutchman's pipe, clematis climbs by twining, so give it a trellis or wire support. Clematis vines need sun to flower well, but prefer to have cold feet; mulch their roots or protect them by planting a low-growing ground cover. The hybrid clematis vines have the showiest flowers, but some species, like sweet autumn clematis (*C. paniculata*), are hardier and better for screening. Sweet autumn is a robust vine covered with scented white flowers in late August, and with plumy seed heads in the fall.

Trumpet creeper (*Campsis radicans*) is another good choice. It bears two-inch-wide, orange-scarlet trumpet-shaped flowers in midsummer. Since it climbs by means of small clinging rootlets, you needn't worry about trellising, at least when the vine is young. Be sure you really want this vine; once planted, trumpet creeper can be extremely tenacious.

Gardeners in need of quick color and screening can plant annual vines, some of which grow almost as fast as Jack's beanstalk. Moonflower (*Ipomoea alba*) reaches fifteen feet and bears enormous, fragrant white flowers that open in the evening. Morning glory, another *Ipomoea*, is a popular choice and comes in a heavenly blue, among other colors.

No porch is complete without a hanging basket or two, perhaps filled with impatiens or tuberous begonias. My favorite hanging plant is a fuchsia. Fuchsias like shelter and shade — just what your porch provides. I think the intricate flowers are best appreciated close up, say from the vantage of a comfortable rocker with a glass of cool lemonade in hand.

WINDOW BOXES

When I think of window boxes, I think of Europe. Even in crowded cities, most Europeans find a spot for some flowers. Cascades of bright bloom hang from nearly every windowsill. In our own country, more people are discovering the charm of gardening in window boxes or hanging pots.

There's a big difference between growing plants in window boxes and growing them in the ground. In a window box, the soil dries out quickly and in warm weather can get hot enough to damage plant roots. The more soil you put in your window box, the better plants will be protected. But a big box full of soil is heavy. So try for a happy medium — no pun intended. A box ten inches front to back and eight inches deep with a lightweight, soilless planting mix will help keep the weight down.

You can get window boxes in a variety of materials, including metal, plastic, fiberglass, and wood. Metal's inexpensive, but it rusts and conducts heat, making soil even hotter in summer. Plastic and fiberglass boxes don't conduct heat and are usually moderately priced and lightweight.

Wood doesn't conduct heat but needs to be treated with a preservative, unless it's naturally decay resistant like redwood or cedar. The safest wood preservatives for home gardeners to apply are copper naphthanate and zinc naphthanate. Avoid chemicals like creosote and pentachlorophenol. Commercially pressure-treated lumber is generally safe for garden plants since little of the arsenic compounds used in this treatment leach into the soil. Make sure you wear a dust mask if you saw pressure-treated wood, though.

It's surprising how many window boxes have no drainage holes. If yours don't, drill some holes in the bottom to prevent root damage from soggy soil. A soilless peat-perlite planting mix not only is lightweight but drains beautifully. Garden earth in a window box doesn't. If you use garden soil, mix it with peat moss, perlite, or vermiculite to help it drain well. Any planting mix in a window box will dry out quickly, so plan to water frequently. With all that water washing nutrients out of the soil, you should fertilize every two or three weeks with a houseplant fertilizer, diluted to about half the recommended strength. Plants in a soilless mix will need to be fertilized more often than those in soil.

Choosing plants for your window box is fun. If it will get at least six hours of sun, you have lots of choices. Geraniums, marigolds, and petunias are the classic window box plants. A favorite of mine is vinca, which seems to thrive even with rather erratic care. Tuberous begonias, impatiens, wax begonias, and coleus work in shady conditions. Lobelia makes a nice addition to a window box provided it's placed in light shade. For boxes in *really* deep shade, try ferns or English ivy. Or you can let plants take turns in sun and shade. Put them in individual pots within the different window boxes and surround the pots with damp peat moss so they don't dry out. Then switch those in deep shade and those in sun with each other, every week.

If you're really dedicated, you can keep color in your window boxes nearly all year. In early spring plant pansies, perhaps along with some potted miniature daffodils. Later replace the daffodils with annuals that will bloom all summer. When fall comes, fill the boxes with chrysanthemums. Follow the mums with evergreen branches, enlivened with some sprays of bittersweet for color.

Window boxes filled with live plants say "welcome" much more warmly than a welcome mat at the front door, and they cheer every passerby.

─── ◦ 11 ◦ ───
Old-Fashioned Flowers

COLUMBINE

When I was young and soda fountains were still the popular gathering spots for teens, sodas and sundaes were always served in what we called "tulip glasses." They were thick, footed glasses with deeply scalloped tops — it was easy to rest two straws (or even four if your group ran out of change) in the indentations in a single glass.

Columbines (*Aquilegia*), as well as tulips, remind me of those glasses. The columbine bloom is narrow, deep, and sharply scalloped; only the narrow spurs that project above the petals don't fit the soda glass picture — but they do add to the flowers' beauty. The delicate tints of the blooms (mine run from cream to pinkish-lavender) are enchanting.

What's surprising, knowing Nature as we do, is that she

doesn't make us battle to produce these lovely, intricate flowers. They're so adaptable she sprinkles them everywhere. Native American columbines grow on our mountains, hillsides, and wooded land. I've seen them nodding from gravelly roadside banks that look as forbidding as a desert, and wondered what on earth they're finding for nourishment.

It's easiest to start columbine seeds outdoors, in light or sandy soil that's well drained. You can plant them any time you want a break from fighting aphids or hoeing weeds. They don't care if it's spring or midsummer; they'll catch hold and give you blooms the next year.

Columbines are also perennial, so you need to plant most of them only once. Some of the newer hybrids, however, seem to be shorter-lived than the older varieties; you may want a mix until you see how long they survive in your garden. If you remove columbines' faded flowers before they go to seed, you may be able to extend the blooming season by several weeks. Both flowers and fernlike foliage keep well when cut and added to bouquets. Don't worry if the original plants die out after a few years. Provided you haven't cut all of your columbine flowers, they'll have self-seeded, so the bed should continue to produce.

Columbines must have at least half a day of sunshine during spring. After that they don't mind partial shade all day. They're hardy enough to survive cold winters in nearly all of the country.

You can buy dwarf columbines with flowers no more than an inch or so across, or you can buy standards or even giant hybrids with blossoms the size of demitasse cups. The dwarf plants are likely to be twelve to eighteen inches in height, nice for a narrow flower border. For wide borders, you might try wild columbine (*A. canadensis*), which grows two to four feet tall.

Columbines come in many colors, including red, yellow,

and sky blue. Sky blue Rocky Mountain columbine (*A. caerulea*) is a heavenly flower. Columbines may give you a bonus from the bird world. Hummingbirds like dipping their long beaks into the deep cups of the nectar-rich flowers. The sight of no other bird brings quite the same thrill to my family. When any member of the family calls out *"Ooooh*, hummers!" we all rush to the window. The tiny birds offer one more good reason to grow pink or red columbines: they're the hummers' favorite colors.

FOXGLOVES

What is more quintessentially English than a quaint thatched cottage, its flower-packed garden a riot of color within a white picket fence? I like to indulge in the fantasy of spending a summer in such an idyllic spot, strolling along the garden paths on sunny days, admiring the exuberance of leaf and flower.

The plants one thinks of for a cottage garden are not sophisticated snooty beauties; they're the simpler plants our grandparents grew.

One of my favorites is foxgloves. The lovely spires of these old-fashioned flowers have unpretentious charm. Even their name delights me. I have read that it's a corruption of "folks' glove," the folks being the fairies.

Foxglove (*Digitalis*) is the source of a drug used to treat some heart ailments. All parts of the foxglove are considered poisonous; make sure children never nibble on the leaves.

The most familiar foxgloves are biennials; many of us have them in our gardens. They grow their greenery the first year, then flower and set seed the second year. *D. purpurea*, the foxglove of the English countryside, is one of these. Its spires of purple, bell-shaped flowers reach two to four feet, adding one of the earliest-blooming vertical accents to the flower garden in June and on into July. The Shirley hybrid foxgloves, named after the town in England where they were bred, are large and vigorous, reaching as high as six feet. They have closely clustered blossoms in shades of white, rose, and purple. On the other hand, many gardeners prefer the Excelsior hybrids. Their flowers completely encircle the stems, unlike those of other varieties, which tend to grow on one side only. Excelsior flowers are attached to the stem almost at a right angle, rather than an acute angle, so the spotted markings inside the blossoms are easily visible.

All foxgloves like soil that is well drained and high in organic matter. They do well in full sun or partial shade.

One variety, *D. purpurea* 'Foxy', has been bred to bloom in one season. Even so, it takes five or six months for the plants to reach flowering size, so in cooler areas it's best to plant seeds indoors in January for June bloom.

To grow the other biennial varieties from seed is a longer process. Sow the fine seed in July; overwinter the young plants, preferably in a cold frame; then plant them out the following spring. Or for a foxglove shortcut, find seedlings at your garden center. These year-old plants will blossom that summer. Foxglove seedlings don't take kindly to rough handling; try not to disturb the root ball when you move them to their permanent home. That's easiest if the plants you buy are in individual pots or cells.

Another shortcut is to try perennial foxgloves. *D. grandiflora* has yellow flowers and looks nice in a woodland setting. The strawberry-colored blossoms of *D.* × *mertonensis* are showier, but the plant is not as cold hardy. Although both of these perennials are often short-lived, they will naturalize. While *D.* × *mertonensis* is a hybrid, it comes true from seed. The biennial varieties may also naturalize. However, the naturalized offspring of the hybrids usually don't run true to type, so I just pull them up. Occasionally, offshoots will rise from the base of biennial plants that have finished flowering. These can be left to provide another crop of flowers the following summer.

DIANTHUS

One of my happy garden memories is of walking to a local farmstand in spring to buy a basket of sweet William for the garden. The rectangular splint basket would overflow with young plants in full bloom, newly dug from the field. The blossoms were a riot of colors, from white to pink to deep red. These biennial plants were just beginning their second season, so they were ready to be put in the ground and flower.

These days sweet William (*Dianthus barbatus*) usually comes in plastic flats or pots; the days of splint baskets are long past. But the old-fashioned flower, and many of its dianthus relatives, are still lovely in many gardens.

Dianthus is a big clan, including perennials, annuals, and biennials, ranging from the fussy greenhouse carnation to the charming pinks of English cottage gardens. Carnations and most pinks have a heady, clovelike scent.

My old standby, sweet William, is unlike many of its cousins in that it has no fragrance. Sweet William compensates for this lack by producing large, showy flower heads, each one a bouquet of many small blooms. Plants flower best in spring and early summer, before the weather gets hot. The taller strains reach as much as a foot in height; the low-growing ones make a charming edging for a flower bed.

The flowers called pinks acquired their name not from their color, as I used to believe, but from the fact that the edges of the blossoms look as if they'd been carefully cut out by pinking shears. Today, you can get pinks in white, pink, red, and even yellow; many blossoms have an "eye" of contrasting color.

The grass pink, sometimes called cottage pink (D. plumarius), is a perennial. Growing about a foot high, it blooms in late spring and early summer. Its pert, fringed flowers cover a dense mat of attractive gray-green foliage.

Unfortunately for Southern and Midwestern gardeners, pinks do not take kindly to hot weather. When the mercury rises they stop blooming and tend to be short-lived. Coastal areas offer ideal conditions, but I grow pinks quite successfully in Vermont, on the northwest side of our home. They like slightly alkaline soil, and I make sure they have good drainage — they don't like wet feet. In winter I mulch them.

Early in this century a British nurseryman first bred the Allwood pinks, considered to be a cross between cottage pinks and the perpetual-flowering carnation. Allwood crosses (D. Allwoodii) provide the compactness of pinks with the generous blooming of carnations.

The perennial maiden pink (D. deltoides) is lovely in rock gardens. It can spread to form a mat several feet across. You can get pink, red, or white varieties, though they're not fragrant. Maiden pink blooms in late spring and early summer. Another good rock garden or ground cover choice is the Cheddar pink (D. gratianopolitanus), named for the part of England where it grows. It too spreads enthusiastically, and its blooms are scented.

Among the annual pinks are China pink (D. chinensis) and Deptford pink (D. armenia). Start them from seed about eight weeks before setting out. Annual pinks like full sun and fairly cool summers; in hot areas, put them where there's some afternoon shade. New varieties are fairly heat-resistant and should give you beautiful blooms nearly all summer. If they slow down, shear them back to bloom again when cooler weather returns.

POPPIES

They blaze in a garden near ours every year; their translucent petals catch the sun and glow like flames. No other plants can quite match the flamboyance of Oriental poppies in full bloom. Bold and handsome, these old-fashioned flowers steal the show in late spring and early summer.

Here in Vermont, just about every old farmhouse has a clump or two of perennial Oriental poppies in the yard. Most have vivid scarlet blooms rising above gray-green foliage. Red's the traditional poppy color, but there are plenty of other choices, too. There are shades of salmon and pink; there's even a pure white poppy. Many varieties have dark spots at the base of their petals. I like having color choices, because flame red isn't an easy color to place well in the garden, especially in cases where it has orange overtones. These show-offs need a background with lots of neutral color, like green foliage plants or possibly white flowers. If you want to create an intense, eye-catching picture, try vermilion Oriental poppies with deep violet-blue salvia.

Poppies live long and are hardy. They like to be divided every five years or so, but they're so broad-minded they'll flower acceptably even if you make them wait longer. They're not fussy about soil so long as it's well drained. In the North, they like full sun; in the South, it is a good idea to give them some light shade in the hot afternoon. Gardeners in the deep South, where winters stay warm, can't get poppies to thrive, unfortunately; but as they can grow many exotic and colorful flowers that won't live where winters are cold, maybe it all balances out.

In midsummer, poppies undergo a change of personality that would send weaker characters rushing to a psychiatrist. They go from show-off to self-effacing; their tops simply dry up and disappear, leaving a gap in the flower garden. Many people plant baby's breath among their poppies, so big drifts of those tiny flowers will fill in the empty space.

Poppies self-sow with abandon. Be sure to remove blooms before they go to seed, unless you want them all over the place next year — and all red, as they usually revert to that color even if the parent hybrid was a more delicate color.

Most Oriental poppies are sold as plants, not seeds, because the seeds of hybrids don't duplicate the parental traits exactly. To get new poppy plants identical to the plants you grow, divide the clumps in midsummer after the foliage has died down but before new growth appears.

In my day, schoolchildren were required to memorize the World War I poem that begins "In Flanders fields the poppies blow/Between the crosses, row on row." We were taught that the flowers glowing amid the crosses were symbols of hope for the future. To this day I feel a glow of optimism when I look at the bright, saucy faces of red poppies.

SUNFLOWERS

The rose, with its delicate, soft beauty and rainbow of colors, is our official national flower.

But there is another flower, far from delicate, but sturdy, tall, tough, wholesome, and of superb geometric design, that perhaps should be the unofficial symbol of America. It's ubiquitous, handsome, and edible, and was as popular among the Native Americans centuries ago as it is with the rest of us today. And it's a native American itself: the sunflower.

In its wild state the sunflower plant produces dozens and dozens of showy heads. The popular domesticated version of *Helianthus annuus* forms a single stalk, thick as a young tree trunk, topped by a golden face in a tiara of yellow petals; its face follows the bright sun as the day progresses.

Like the American eagle, it makes a handsome symbol of strength and endurance. It's also useful. American Indians learned that sunflower seeds were a rich source of food. It was they who eventually domesticated these plants.

Sunflowers went from here to Europe, in time reaching Russia. They have become such an important crop plant there that some people mistakenly think they must be native to that country. By 1616 sunflowers were fairly common in England, where herbalists said they produced stalks "of the bignesse of a strong man's armes." They reported, perhaps a little wistfully, that the plants grew to a height of twenty-four feet in Spain; the tallest in England were fourteen feet.

When they first saw the plants, European herbalists tested them for medicinal value. They couldn't find any. It wasn't until the next century that the food value of the tasty seeds became widely understood in Europe.

At least two sunflowers are often not recognized as such. There's one native to Texas, the cucumber-leaf sunflower (*H. debilis cucumerifolius*), which looks like a kind of black-eyed Susan. It has many small flowers with dark centers and creamy petals. Related to the cucumber-leaf sunflower is the beach sunflower of coastal Florida. Fussy as a millionaire, this plant grows on only the very best beaches from Marineland to Miami Beach. It grows prostrate, its long stems parallel to the ground. It is so attractive that many Florida gardeners have transplanted large numbers of the plants as ornamentals in their yards.

There are many species of sunflower, and many color variations. You can find magenta, orange, yellow, mixed shades, and double forms that make lovely ornamental arrangements.

I heard a story once about a Briton who immigrated to

Colorado and there bred one of the loveliest sunflowers, a true red.

One summer day in 1910, a Mrs. Cockerell told her husband she'd seen what she thought was a lovely red butterfly in a field near the house. When it didn't fly away, and she went closer to investigate, she found it was a red sunflower. The Cockerells carefully dug it up and transplanted it to their yard. They eventually developed a true-breeding red sunflower; they sold seeds to an English company, and in time their red sunflowers traveled around the world.

When the Cockerell family visited Russia in 1932 they were pleased to see their red sunflowers (*H. annuus* 'Russian Giant') gracing a public park. They talked with the park director about the flowers, telling him a bit of their history. He listened, then said simply, "This is not your sunflower. This is the Red Sunflower of the Red Army."

──o 12 o──
Problem Solvers to the Rescue

MORNING GLORIES

When we moved into our present home, one of the things that bothered me most was the overpowering presence of the garage. It's big, and in those early days before we'd done any landscaping, its broad, blank wooden walls were a lot more noticeable than the house was.

We couldn't do much about the side of the garage where the cars (and the lawn mowers, tiller, and other tools) made their entrances and exits, or the side facing the breezeway entrance. But we could do something, quickly, about the two remaining walls.

We needed things that would grow upward to hide those broad expanses. We wanted low-care plants, too, because we knew we'd have our hands full turning our acre of space into lawns and gardens.

On one long garage wall we started Concord grapevines, and it turned out to be one of the smartest things we ever did. We never have to give them any help except for occasional severe but unscientific pruning, yet they give us grapes every year, sometimes in such quantity we could keep Bacchus supplied.

On the southwest side of the garage I wanted to have a little kitchen garden bed, so whatever climber I chose for the garage wall couldn't be as heavy and space-grabbing as grapevines. I put a dozen lengths of string from the bottom to the top of the wall, attached to nails I'd hammered into the siding. Then I planted morning glories (*Ipomoea nil*) in the ground near each bottom nail.

It worked like a charm. The morning glories made a beautiful display behind the lettuces and cherry tomatoes. The Northeast is a good area for morning glories because they usually winterkill and therefore can't spread as a weed into neighbors' yards. I understand in some of the far Western states, regulations won't permit gardeners to raise these lovely flowers, they're so rambunctious.

Morning glory seeds are hard as little bricks, so I scarified them before planting — just took a knife and made cuts in the outer covering to help the embryo plant break loose. If you try morning glories, wait for warm weather to plant them; to grow well, they like the soil to reach at least fifty degrees. Even with a fairly late start, say June, they bloom all through August and September.

My simple strings are perfectly adequate for these cheery climbers, because the vines are very light. The flowers open early in the morning, their colors making our garage wall downright pretty. When the hot noontime sun beats down, the blooms close; hence their name. They brighten our many cloudy days, all day long. My family was thrilled to find that hummingbirds like morning glories. It's entrancing to watch these tiny creatures dip their slender bills into the morning glory hearts; the birds' wings are a blur of motion, their bright colors glowing in the sunshine.

Of course morning glories will grow on any fence or trellis; once they're about six inches high, they start looking for something to grab. If you want to screen an area for privacy, you can lay down a wood base, then attach either wire or string to nails hammered in it at intervals of your choice. Tie the other end of the string to an upper wire connected to corner posts. The morning glories will climb as high as twelve feet, making living walls.

These white, blue, red, or lavender blossoms are well named. They were certainly the glory of my mornings, in those early days when our landscape consisted mostly of weedy grass and blank walls.

THE GOATSBEARD SOLUTION

It sounds like the title of a spy novel — but for me and a friend, goatsbeard *was* a solution, not to a mystery but to a gardening challenge.

My friend has a small garden bed, eight by six feet, running along the walk to her front door. It doesn't have to look stunning all season, but it does need to look presentable, preferably without too much effort. The planting has to be high enough to hide the foundation of the porch behind it. But it was tough to choose plants for this spot because of its northeast exposure, very little direct sun, and quite moist soil.

I had fun one afternoon leafing through my garden books in search of suitable candidates. And when I came across the inelegantly named goatsbeard I thought I had found the answer. Goatsbeard (*Aruncus dioicus*) is a perennial of many virtues which deserves more widespread use. Large and shrublike, it bears graceful plumes of cream-colored flowers in early summer. Looking something like a giant astilbe, goatsbeard is a good accent plant. The compound leaves remain attractive all season long. No fussy prima donna, goatsbeard will thrive in a variety of soils, but does best in moist soil that is high in organic matter, and in part shade. Long-lived, usually untroubled by pests and diseases, rarely needing division or staking — it seemed to be just what I was looking for. The only drawback was its size — five to six feet tall, with a three- to four-foot spread, goatsbeard would overwhelm the small bed my friend needed to fill.

Fortunately, goatsbeard has some relatives of more modest growth. The goatsbeard *A. dioicus* 'Kneiffi' has the same good looks and easy habits as its larger parent, but grows to only three feet tall and a foot and a half wide. Its more finely cut foliage is in keeping with its smaller scale.

There is an even smaller goatsbeard — with an even larger name, *A. aesthusifolius*. This little plant reaches a mere nine to twelve inches, making it a lovely edging plant for a shaded border. Like its larger relations, it shows off its spires of white flowers in early summer.

Goatsbeard is so pretty, my friend decided to have both of the smaller varieties in her garden. The completed plan for the bed includes ferns in the background; low-growing pulmonaria for its spring flowers and speckled foliage; astilbe to echo the form and flowers of the goatsbeard and add a deep rose accent; and turtlehead (*Chelone*), whose pink blossoms add a spot of color in late summer and early fall. All of these plants enjoy their independence; give them moist soil and partial shade and they'll grow nicely whether you're there or not.

UNDER-TREE GROWERS

When I was young I remember my aunt slaving every year to make a lawn in her front yard. Each spring she got advice from well-meaning neighbors and spent a lot of her time and money dumping stuff on the bare earth — sand to lighten the soil, fertilizer, peat moss, grass seed, and so on. The grass never grew. Eventually she moved away. A few years ago I drove by the old house and discovered the current owners had finally figured out how to grow a thriving lawn — they cut down the Norway maple that had stood in the middle of the yard.

What my aunt never realized was that in the struggle to make a lawn she was competing with a powerful adversary —that tree. It is quite impossible to grow a lawn beneath a large Norway maple, with its dense shade and shallow, greedy roots.

Not all trees are as difficult to deal with. Honey locusts cast an open shade under which a respectable lawn will grow. Oaks and apple trees are deep-rooted; if you prune them to keep them fairly open, they can be good lawn companions. But Norway maples, silver maples, horse chestnuts, and beeches are despots about their own territory.

If you have such a tree in your yard, are you doomed to bare earth? Not necessarily. True, there are some situations where nothing, not even weeds, will grow. So just spread bark mulch under the tree and stop worrying. But if the gloom under your tree is somewhat less intense, you can probably get green growth, if not a lawn.

Siberian bugloss is a wonderful shade plant that can survive somewhat dry, shady conditions. Its name isn't pretty, but the plant has heart-shaped leaves and delicate forget-me-not blue flowers that are inspired to bloom in April and May. The Latin name, a bit more respectable than "bugloss," is *Brunnera macrophylla*, a name you might prefer to use when showing off your shade garden to friends and neighbors.

Many gardeners swear by hostas as shade plants. You can get them with tiny leaves or leaves as big as lunch plates; you can get them with green leaves of varying tints, some edged with white; or you can choose those with golden leaves. Most people grow them for their lovely foliage, but their flowers in white, lavender, or purple are handsome, too.

Ground covers are often more suitable for shady situations than most other plants. The trouble is that the conditions under your tree may be not simply shady, but dry and nutrient-poor as well, thanks to shallow tree roots. What you need is something that looks good but is really tough.

Ground covers are a great boon, but they aren't quite maintenance-free. (Nothing is, except plastic geraniums, and even those have to be dusted.) Ground covers need the most attention while they're getting established; later they become thick enough to choke out weeds.

Epimediums are among my favorite ground cover plants. They'll tolerate dry shady conditions. Their heart-shaped foliage is their main claim to fame, but their spurred flowers are delicate and lovely in spring.

The most common name for epimediums is "bishop's hat"; that's because each blossom is shaped like a biretta, a hat worn by the Catholic clergy. You don't hear epimediums' other common name, barrenwort, as often. That name comes from the fact that one species of epimedium was confused with another plant, whose roots were supposed to help in birth control. Whatever you call them, epimediums are a good choice for the gardener who wants low-maintenance plants. If you want to increase your supply of epimediums, all you need to do is divide them.

One thing to remember is that not all epimediums are

equally good ground covers. Some, while they're charming to look at, don't spread. That may recommend them for some situations, but the species that spread fairly rapidly by rhizomes are the ones to give you a carpet of green.

Epimedium × *versicolor* is one of my favorites. It spreads fast, but it's not invasive. Once established, it's dense enough to keep weeds down. The young leaves are marked with red; later they turn solid green and are attractive all season long. The flowers rise above the foot-high foliage, so you can enjoy their delicate beauty from a distance. The most common strain is *E.* × *versicolor* 'Sulphureum'. Its flowers are a lovely combination of two shades of yellow. It's a semievergreen whose leaves persist through the winter, but get pretty ragged by spring. I clip it to the ground before snow flies, so the old foliage won't cover up new spring growth.

Another species that does well as a ground cover is *E. pinnatum*. It also spreads rapidly, forming a dense mat of semievergreen leaves that wear a crown of yellow flowers in spring. *E.* × *rubrum* probably puts on the best spring show of all. Its large crimson flowers have creamy accents, and an established clump is a cloud of blooms in spring. *E.* × *rubrum* isn't a spreader, but if you plant closely, it makes a ground cover of sorts for a small area. For super bloom, though, give it more elbow room and it will become a showpiece.

Another hardy ground cover that can live beneath most trees is silveredge goutweed — *Aegopodium podagraria* 'Variegatum', also called bishop's weed. Be warned: this plant can become an invasive weed under good growing conditions. But in situations where nothing else seems to thrive, goutweed is often the answer. Its leaves are beautifully splashed with white, so they're very attractive in a shady spot. Goutweed grows about a foot tall. In summer it produces white flowers that somewhat resemble Queen

Anne's lace, but they are sparse; the leaves are the main attraction.

Other possibilities for ground covers in shady areas are ajuga, or bugleweed, which forms a low mat of lustrous green leaves with spikes of blue flowers in spring; and the old standbys, pachysandra and myrtle. I have also found lily of the valley to be an adaptable ground cover and have an abundant supply under an oak tree.

No matter what you are growing, do what you can to make the conditions as suitable as possible. If your tree is small enough, a little judicious pruning may let enough light through the canopy to give you a broader range of choices of plants to grow below. And because the plants underneath are competing with the tree roots, remember to water and fertilize more frequently than you would otherwise.

---- ∘ 13 ∘ ----

The Carrot
Caper

Sometimes I think I've learned as much from gardening as I did from school. I remember some years ago when the garden taught me a simple, practical lesson in plant care. My daughter and I walked out one Saturday morning, early in the gardening season, just to look at the family's four gardens and see what needed doing most. We'd had ample rain, so we could easily pull a weed here and there as we walked.

After a bit I noticed what appeared to be a row of planted, assorted weeds near the fence around one garden. It looked as if we had planted a packet of Page's Superior Weed Mix. We went over to check it out. Hiding among the sturdy weeds was an overwhelmed row of new carrots everybody'd forgotten about. (When parents work and kids are in school, there's always *something* that gets overlooked.) Without much optimism, my daughter and I assumed the Gardener's Kneel and started hand weeding.

No gloves — this was very delicate work. The carrots were so young, they were just wisps of thready two-inch roots with tiny feather tops, gasping for a breath of air and a ray of sunshine. Every time we pulled up a weed, several carrot plants came with it. With great care, we tucked each one back into the warm earth, though they looked so feeble we weren't at all confident about their future. Nonetheless, it was a fine day, the sun was warm on our backs, and it was a superb chance to have a real visit with each other while doing something that just might turn out to be useful.

The carrot row was more than thirty feet long, so it took us hours to complete the job. As we inched along, we tossed all the weeds into a big basket. When we finished, we had a huge harvest of pigweed, lamb's-quarters, Johnsongrass, dandelions, and aching backs, all for a pathetic row of droopy little green carrot tops flopped on the ground. We wondered whether we'd wasted our time, but we watered the poor little things carefully anyhow.

The next day I looked at the row and thought the plants seemed a bit perkier. Then for three days we were all so busy we forgot the carrots. Late in the week, my husband and I took our courage in our hands and went to the garden where (please, please) the carrots might be growing. And they were! It was like a miracle. Half dead when we started weeding, almost all pulled up and replaced — and now look how grateful those carrots were.

My way of showing my appreciation was to give those carrots extra care the rest of the summer. It was easy to keep them weed-free: our hand weeding had brought no new weed seeds to the surface, and the row was so clean it was simple to pull out the few weed sprigs that turned up now and then in our immaculate row. I thinned the carrots as needed, and gave them fish emulsion when I had to water them in early August. Their bed had plenty of compost, and I put more along both sides of the row in case they needed it. Let me tell you, that summer the Page family had the most beautiful, long, straight, orange carrots we've ever enjoyed.

The lesson we took to heart is that plants *want* to grow; they'll do their darnedest for you, given half a chance. Because weed plants are the bullies on the block and grow faster than young crops, we try to keep ahead of them. But if we don't, and are forced to perform an emergency rescue mission, our flowers and food plants are quite likely to hang in there and grab a new hold on the earth.

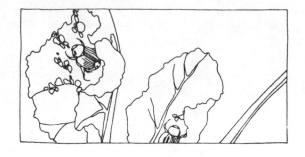

—○ 14 ○—

Beetles
and Other Bugs

THE GOOD, THE BAD, AND THE UGLY

Everything in the world is fascinating to a baby. Babies of crawling age will pick up an ant or a breadcrumb, a bit of carpet fluff or a beetle, with the same curiosity — and often with the same result. They eat it.

The very young find both crawling and flying insects attractive; bugs are toys that move with a will of their own. Children's prejudices against bugs, which often develop by the age of three or four, come from us. I learned that one day when my first child was only a year and a half old. I was down on the floor with a dust mop, reaching way under a bed. My daughter toddled up to me with a happy smile and held out right under my nose the biggest cockroach I've ever seen. I was careful not to say a word, but my face must have reflected my feelings all too clearly. Within a split second she had hurled the insect away from her with a shudder and burst into a storm of tears.

I still react with revulsion to some bugs, especially fat, squishy ones. But as a gardener, I know I'd do better to make them useful to me. Why can't I look upon them as a lesson from Nature? Can't I force the insects themselves to teach me a bit of entomology, if I watch their life cycles and behavior? After observing them closely for a long enough time, I'll undoubtedly learn a lot more about how to control the bad guys and encourage the good guys than I know now.

I must try to see each insect as a specimen for study, not just an interloper. In fact, I've already tried this to some extent. When I first noticed through observation that the imported cabbageworm produces several generations in one season, I realized I'd have to be vigilant all summer long. We use the natural control, *Bacillus thuringiensis* (popularly known as Bt), several times during the season.

Hardest of all is to force yourself to salvage a lesson out of complete disaster. One year, Mexican bean beetles had an orgy in our bean patch, turning healthy plants into skeletons. But by the time the attack was over, our family had seen those beetles at every stage in their life cycle. The next year we knew just where to look for the eggs and started crushing them as soon as they began appearing on the undersides of leaves. We couldn't get every one, but we'd learned from observation that the larvae are yellowish gray and spotted. We were therefore able to destroy any bean beetles that reached the larval stage.

Now consider the big black beetles we sometimes see in our gardens. Since childhood, when our older brother used to try to scare my sister and me by threatening to put them down our backs, I've found them offensive. I've even purposely stepped on some in the garden.

Not any more. As soon as I realized that nearly all ground

beetles are predators, I started apologizing to them for getting in their way, and walked carefully around them. They kill some of our worst pests — cutworms, cankerworms, and gypsy moth larvae. Now, I even take time to admire the way the light glints off their shining dark armor as they clamber busily about among the pebbles and little clods of earth.

Most useful in our gardens are the ladybird beetle; the carrion beetles, the natural world's janitors, whose name describes their food; rove beetles, which also eat decaying vegetable matter; and some scarab beetles, such as the dung beetle. Not all scarabs are helpful, though — our old enemy the Japanese beetle is a scarab. Additional predators of harmful garden insects include the tiger, stinkbug, soldier, firefly, and checkered beetles, as well as the soft-winged flower beetles. One bug I'd like to see in action is called the bombardier beetle. When threatened, it shoots out a little cloud of nasty-smelling liquid, simultaneously making an explosive sound like a tiny popgun. It can do this several times running, as if its ambition were to be a miniature machine gun.

Other "good" insects include firefly larvae, called glowworms. They eat snails and slugs, bless their pretty little lights. And Western gardeners, often troubled by grasshoppers and locusts, might appreciate the blister beetle in one of its two forms: the larvae consume grasshopper eggs and other soil insects. (Unfortunately, the adult beetles gourmandize on plant foliage.)

Among the bad beetles in the garden are larvae of click beetles; they're those horrid little wireworms that eat crop roots and tubers. You can identify click beetles easily: turn a beetle over on its back, and if it promptly flips itself into the air, hoping to land right side up, it's a clicker. Weevils may be the most destructive group, at least so far as gardeners are concerned; this group includes the snout beetle and the curculios that attack our tree fruits.

I've decided the best thing we gardeners can do when we come across an insect we can't identify is to leave it alone; then get out the bug book and look it up. I hope never again to destroy any critter that's helping to control pests and tidy up decaying materials in or near my garden.

FLEA BEETLES

Flea beetles are a pain in the neck. We've been lucky in the Page garden — we've had only one really serious flea beetle attack in some years, but it taught us a lesson. One summer they got into our cabbage patch, which we hadn't watched closely because it was set off by itself. The cabbages were next to a weedy field, and I realized (too late) that that made it easier for the bugs to infiltrate. When I visited the garden one day to see whether some of the cabbages were pickable, the poor things looked as if they'd been used for BB shot practice.

It'd be quicker to list plants flea beetles won't attack than those they do. They go for just about all the usual garden vegetables, plus grapevines and apple and plum trees. Sometimes the damage the beetles do isn't serious; mature, healthy plants can survive a few holes in their leaves. But the adult beetles — although only a tenth of an inch long, maximum, at maturity — can devour emerging seedlings.

In spring, you need to check young plants for flea beetles every few days or so. Look at both tops and undersides of leaves. If you see some little dots and aren't sure what they are, place a white tissue next to a leaf with dots on it. Jiggle the plant. If small dark spots hop onto the tissue, then quickly hop off, they're flea beetles, all right. Doesn't take them long to recognize what's inedible.

The worst thing about flea beetles is that they make garden havoc a family enterprise. While the parents chomp away at the leaves above ground, the larvae of some species masticate underground stems, seeds, and roots. The larvae are narrow, whitish, and a quarter-inch long, not easy to spot. Their damage is obvious, though. If some of your plants look sickish for no apparent reason, dig a couple of them out and look for evidence of larvae chewing away at their roots. The best way to keep the larvae away from the plants is to keep the seedlings covered with netted row covers. This will keep out the adults and thus the larvae. You can also apply a soil insecticide. If you want to do this, get advice from your Cooperative Extension agent.

When the larvae attack potatoes, you can see their off-color "tracks" as well as black spots under the potato skins. If you've had a problem with flea beetles in corn in the past, from now on plant one of the resistant varieties available through garden catalogs. Flea beetles don't care where you live — there are a dozen or more varieties of flea beetles in various colors, and they're found in every region. As a group, they're so smorgasbord-minded they'll subsist on weeds until your succulent young plants appear. That makes one means of control obvious — keep the garden tidy. Remove all debris in autumn, uproot those weeds around the garden fence, and cultivate well again in spring to bring any larvae to the surface where they'll be exposed to the elements.

If you have a flea beetle problem one year, plant as late as you can the next year. That way there's a good chance most of the larvae will die of starvation before you plant. New-hatched flea beetle larvae are *not* among the mouths you want your garden to feed. You could also try floating plastic row covers over seedlings and young transplants. They let in air, light, and moisture, but not flea beetles.

Flea beetles will make a beetle-line for any water-stressed young plants. Keep your plants healthy with ample moisture, good drainage, plenty of nutrients, and excellent weed control. Plants under even moderate stress may surrender quickly to pest attacks. Healthy plants are gutsier; they'll often give you a respectable harvest in spite of a flea beetle invasion.

Help! Japanese beetles have descended upon our roses, which seem to be their favorites, and also on just about everything else in the garden that attracts their fancy — they drive me mad! I don't know whether it's more satisfying, or more disgusting, that I so often can get rid of two at a time because they always seem to be mating. The bug book says they mate only in early summer; all I can say is, the ones at our place never read the book. When I see the lace tatting those beetles make of our flower, vegetable, and grape leaves, I have no compunction about using the heavy artillery.

It's been many years since my husband and I used milky spore disease powder to control the Japanese beetles in our lawn and gardens. Last summer was the first time in ages we saw beetles in any numbers at all. This summer we'll treat our soil again, though the books say that milky spore needs to be applied only once in most circumstances.

Milky spore is a type of bacterium (*Bacillus popilliae*) which affects the larvae of Japanese beetles and some other species of white grubs. The female beetles lay eggs in the soil in July and August; larvae burrow into the soil and feed on decaying vegetation, grass roots, and other roots. When full grown, these larvae are fat, white, and nearly an inch long, curled in an arc. With milky spore disease in the soil, these grubs contract the disease and die. The spores lie dormant in the soil even after all the larvae are destroyed, so they'll be on hand if another invasion occurs.

It takes two to five years to get good control through the milky spore, and it's best if you can get your neighbors to apply it on their lawns at the same time. It's almost pointless to add milky spore to soil already treated with a chemical insecticide, because live grubs are needed to help the spore become established in the soil. As soon as the spore is ingested by the grubs it begins to grow and multiply, thus covering the whole lawn. Once you've added milky spore to the soil, though, it begins to work immediately and remains active for many years thereafter.

While you wait for the spore to become fully effective, you can control the adult Japanese beetles with traps. Pheromone traps attract males; food traps lure the females. A good bait for the adult beetles is fruit cocktail — they love it. Put the traps some distance from the plants you're protecting; you don't want to end up with more beetles on the roses.

Of course these green and bronze beetles have an unfair advantage because they can fly, so you're not likely to get all of them even with a combination of controls. But you'll get hundreds; and having a live army to keep the battle going, in the form of your milky spore bacilli, evens up the odds a bit for the gardener.

SLUGS

Yuk. It didn't surprise me a bit to learn that slimy little garden slugs are related to the octopus and the giant sea squid. They certainly have the appetite of those cousins when they get going on the lettuce and cabbages.

Slugs derive from the same original ancestors as snails — at one time, they had shells. While we know real snails drive West Coast gardeners crazy, at least there's something attractive about their delicate ceramic houses; and snails are edible. There's a growing number of Western gardeners who raise snails for the gourmet market and find it highly profitable. But that's another story.

The naked Eastern slug has only one protection — its mantle, an area of folded skin that it can duck its head back into when necessary. Slugs move by rippling their one flat foot over a layer of mucus, leaving a shiny trail of slime that's readily visible. They'll eat just about anything from strawberries to garbage to animal feces.

What can we do about them in the garden? First, don't expect to eradicate them one hundred percent, you'll only get frustrated. Like fruit flies, they seem to support the theory of spontaneous generation. One day there are none anywhere, the next day your lettuces have become fully tenanted slug condos. The best you can do is try to keep their numbers under control. Slugs contain a great deal of water. Drying out kills them. When it's hot and windy, they hide under anything they can find — stones, plants, bits of wood — to stay moist. They're most active after rain or during fog. Their idea of heaven is a moist, warm night.

A fiendish and good control method is to lure your slug enemies to hiding places you provide, making it easy to kill them. Just lay half-grapefruit shells or overturned cabbage leaves, like little igloos, near infested plants. Flat boards in garden paths work too. Each morning go out, turn over these slug motels and kill the slug conventions being held under them. If you can't face stepping on the squishy things, pour boiling water over them or shake salt on them. Either way they'll die. We've heard from some gardeners who actually get out flashlights and tweezers and wage night war. In the dark, they get their small weapons, search out the slugs in the flashlight beams, and pick them off the plants. Those who do this report there's a certain satisfaction in catching the thieves in the act.

Some gardeners battle slugs with beer. They put throwaway aluminum pie plates in the ground, the rims slightly above ground level, and fill them with stale beer. The slugs creep in, ingest the alcohol, and drown. It helps to cut the plate rim into sharp points and turn them inward. The slugs can easily slide in to drink, but those that imbibe only moderately won't be able to climb out again seeking your garden crudités. If you have an extremely serious problem you can't manage in any other way, you may want to resort to metaldehyde bait. I don't recommend metaldehyde because it's toxic, and you have to be sure it's placed where children and pets can't get at it. It kills the slugs by dehydration. There are other slug baits on the market also.

If worse comes to worst, it's reassuring to know that slugs rarely wipe out a crop. We've often had to take some of the outer leaves off cabbages and sacrifice some of the lower sprouts on Brussels sprout plants because of holes made by slugs, but even when we have slugs by the dozens, we don't lose much of our harvest.

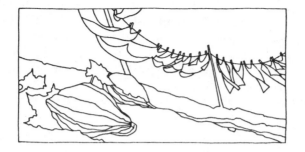

∘ 15 ∘

Old Mother Hubbard

Old Mother Hubbard went to the cupboard
And gave her last name to a squash;
It heightened her fame, as until then her name,
Had only been linked to the wash.

The way a plant is named is often linked to an individual, possibly the one who discovered it or who developed a hybrid. But the Hubbard squash came by its name in a unique way. In the nineteenth century, J. J. Gregory, a superb gardener and seed saver, started a seed company in the Boston area. Here, in his own words, is how it came about that he dubbed a huge, blue-green winter squash the Hubbard. In 1867 he wrote:

It is now about twenty years since this variety was brought to our attention by our old washerwoman, named Hubbard. The squash was brought into Marblehead by a market-man some sixty years ago. . . . To distinguish this squash from a blue variety we were raising, we called it Ma'am Hubbard's Squash. When the seeds became a commercial article, and it became necessary to give it a fixed name, I called it the Hubbard Squash.

If I had been able to forecast its present fame, and had foreseen that it would become the established winter variety, I would have bestowed some more ambitious name on it. But again, I think not, for the old lady was faithful, in her narrow sphere, in her day and generation; a good, humble soul, and it pleases me to think that the name of such an one has become, without any intent of hers, famous.

It's a little surprising that this big, warty, greenish-gray object, hard to hack apart, well known as a space grabber, continues to be grown in many home gardens. But it *is* high in nutrition, and it has a fine, sweet flavor. My favorite winter squashes are Hubbard and butternut, both firm, dry squashes with a sweet taste. They're high in vitamin A and contain an assortment of B vitamins and some phosphorus, potassium, and calcium, so we feel quite virtuous when we're eating them.

Hubbards are garden hogs, though. Gardeners who grow corn can plant their winter squashes in a perimeter around the corn garden; raccoons hate to walk on the prickly vines, so squash plants do double duty. If you can't spare garden space for these big fellows, try some from the market; when fully mature they're good keepers, and they retain their flavor.

Cooking Ma'am Hubbard's squash is simple, assuming you don't grow those giants people show at county fairs. Just put the whole squash in a 350-degree oven until the skin softens and a fork slides smoothly into the flesh. You can cook Hubbards by cutting them up and putting them in boiling water, though they get a bit watery.

Leave the skins on if you do this — peeling them raw is a pain.

My family likes Hubbard squash baked, chunked, and shiningly glazed with butter and brown sugar. Some may think Hubbard squash is a peasant among vegetables, but if so, it needs no glamorizing. It has the peasant's earthy, wholesome quality.

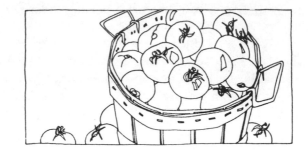

─── ° 16 ° ───

Vegetable
Favorites

TASTIEST TOMATOES

Tomatoes are the most popular home garden crop in America; no doubt it's because the only way you can get a tomato with luscious taste is to grow it yourself. We're lucky to have them, because tomatoes went through a lot before being recognized as gourmet treasures.

They're native to Central and South America, but never got to North America until that indefatigable gardener-statesman, Thomas Jefferson, brought them across the ocean from Europe. Bless the man — always ready to try something new. He grew tomatoes in his famous Monticello gardens after the Revolution and by 1812 they became favorites in the Creole kitchens of New Orleans. Even then, it was a while before everyone was willing to try the fruit; it had a poor reputation for wholesomeness.

What created that reputation? Certainly the Incas of Peru grew and ate tomatoes centuries ago. (Theirs were the little ones we call cherry tomatoes.) But when explorers from Europe brought tomatoes back home, plantspeople realized they belonged to the nightshade family; nightshades are poisonous, so they didn't recommend tomatoes for eating. What may have made matters worse was that handling the plants stained one's hands yellowy-green and made them smell odd.

When first introduced in Europe, the tomato was called *Lycopersicon*, Latin for "wolf peach." That name recognized both the fruits' suspected unwholesomeness and their attractiveness. Soon tomatoes were identified as members of the *Solanaceae* family, known to have almost as many poisonous members as the notorious Borgias. That didn't help inspire confidence in the furry-leaved plants. One of the problems a tomato was supposed to create in its consumers was palpitations of the heart; maybe that's why the French called it *pomme d'amour*, or "love-apple."

It was the Italians of the seventeenth century who first realized the possibilities of the lovely fruits, dubbing them *pomodori*, "apples of gold." Despite the Italian success with the sweet, tart fruits, and despite President Jefferson's later efforts, tomatoes didn't become popular among cautious United States gardeners until a mere hundred years ago. During that single century, though, the fruits have earned their slot at the top of the garden popularity list.

Nowadays gardeners discourse not on tomatoes' edibility, but on how to grow the biggest, tastiest, healthiest ones. There are two schools of thought on special ways to plant tomatoes. Many gardeners favor digging a straight-down, wide, deep hole and filling it with superphosphate, manure, compost, and topsoil in readiness for the young plants. Others swear by the trench method; they dig a long, narrow trench for each plant, put the nutrients in the trench, then lay most of the tomato plant stem along it, with just the upper six to eight inches above the ground.

Since roots form all along the stems in either planting method, I'm not sure the tomatoes care much which way they go in. What they want is lots of water and sunshine, as well as all the goodies the gardener has put into the soil before setting them out.

I had trouble grasping how much water tomatoes like (so long as they are in well-drained soil) until a couple of summers ago when our Vermont garden was rain-drenched much of the time. It was so wet we feared plants might rot. To the contrary, not only tomatoes, but melons, cucumbers, squashes, corn, and just about everything showed an insatiable thirst. Fruits were plentiful, large, and sweet. The only real drawback was that we had a constant battle with hordes of ooky slugs.

Slugs are but one of many enemies serious tomato growers are willing to fight in pursuit of the perfect fruit. Blossom end rot is another. Generous irrigation and mulches can help prevent it. If you can, give your tomatoes either soaker hose or drip irrigation, since wet leaves can set the stage for certain diseases.

Wilt is a tomato disease that offers you no recourse but to uproot and destroy infected plants. However, do not go out on a hot summer afternoon and yank up any tomato plant that droops. It may just be reacting to the sun, and when twilight cools it and dew gives it a drink, the plant may perk right up. If the droop persists, though, chances are your tomato is afflicted with wilt disease and there's no cure. The best prevention is to buy plants labeled VFN. They're resistant to verticillium and fusarium wilts as well as nematodes.

We've been raising tomatoes for thirty-five years, and I'm profoundly impressed by the apparent determination of plants to produce fruits and seeds despite pest and disease attacks. (We always rotate our plantings to prevent disease carry-over and to avoid giving overwintered pests their favorite foods two years running.)

I never tire of the pleasure of going to the garden to pick fresh tomatoes for a meal. Even better is the sensation of biting into a big, luscious fruit right where it's been growing. I lean well over to eat it to the last juicy drop, as I contemplate the super soups and stews these garden favorites will give us next winter.

ELEGANT EGGPLANTS

It's hard to think of a vegetable that comes in as many colors and sizes and is as unusual and beautiful as eggplant. Well, all right, maybe flowering kale. But for me, eggplant, with its deep, glossy sheen, is a notch above kale in aesthetics. Eggplants can be fat and elegantly pear-shaped like Dusky Hybrid; slender and deeply purple like Oriental Ichiban; white, smooth, and perfectly egg-shaped like Easter Egg; or round as baseballs and lavender-striped, like Rosa Bianco. Whatever the variety, the plants are lovely with their pink or lavender golden-hearted flowers.

Actually, eggplant is not a vegetable, it's a berry. Eggplant originated in Asia, and when it first made its way to Europe — as happened with tomatoes — gardeners thought the fruits were poisonous. Fortunately for us, they considered the plants attractive and added them to their flower gardens. Today gardeners can find seed for some of the smaller, more delicate Asian varieties in catalogs.

Of course we don't grow eggplants just for their looks, but they're among the plants that look quite at home in a flower bed; and they aren't hard to grow.

Like their sisters the tomatoes and peppers, eggplants want warm weather, which makes them ideal for the South and West. Northern gardeners, however, can also get a respectable harvest before frost if they start the seeds indoors about eight weeks before planting time. You should harden off young eggplants for about a week before transplanting, giving them a longer time outdoors each of the seven days. If you do this and still can't trust the night temperatures at what should be transplanting time, use cloches or other protection for a week or two. One expert says you can't go wrong if you plant when the iris have finished flowering and the rhododendrons are in bloom; but as some of my iris are still flowering in late June, I'm not sure I trust this formula.

Even if it seems warm when you set out the eggplants, the seventy degrees that feels comfortable to you isn't warm enough to let eggplants relax. It's best to cover the plants with row covers; covers trap warm air around the plants and hold it there at least part way through the cooler nights. Experienced growers say row covers can double your eggplant production. Some Northern growers leave the row covers on all summer, just propping up the sides to let air circulate on hot summer days.

Like Henry VIII, eggplant likes hearty meals on a regular basis. Side-dress at four-week intervals with chemical fertilizer high in phosphorus, or provide lots of organic fertilizer; then be sure the soil is well drained and the plants get good, deep watering regularly. If you happen to get a very hot, dry week, water the eggplant at least twice, deeply.

Eggplants are ripe when their skins take on a glossy shine, but you can pick them as early as you like. Familiar types like Bride, Ichiban, and Farmers Long will grow to twelve inches at maturity; but if you want to pick some at two to three inches, go to it. They're delicious in a mix with other young vegetables. There are also dwarf eggplants that never grow large and can be steamed whole. Small eggplants, whether dwarf or immature, have thin skins and tender flesh. Asian eggplants bruise easily, so cut each one from the plant with a bit of stem intact, then spread the fruits carefully in your harvest basket.

Eggplants are high in fiber and contain a fair amount of potassium, iron, and protein. And a cup of cooked diced eggplant, provided you don't dress it up with any fattening goodies, has only thirty-eight calories. Unfortunately, eggplants don't keep well when fresh — maybe up to a week in the refrigerator.

You can freeze eggplant, though. Breaded slices keep well at zero degrees. Before dipping the slices in the crumbs, salt them and stack them under a plate with a weight atop it until the dark brown juice runs out. Then spread on a pan, quick-freeze, and pack in plastic bags. You can also freeze these summer treats after cooking them up into casseroles with tomatoes and other vegetables. They make elegant one-dish meals served hot over rice on a stormy February day.

We've heard gardeners complain at times that while they like eggplant, they can't get the children to touch it and so it isn't worth the effort of fixing it. They always end up cooking an extra veggie for the young. We used to have this problem, and I solved it with that catchall seasoning, ketchup. I salted the slices lightly, dipped them in breadcrumbs, and sautéed them in a little hot oil. I then spread each slice, edge to edge, with a thin layer of ketchup. It worked like a charm; and once the children got accustomed to accepting eggplant, they learned to eat it in other ways. In a casserole with lamb, rice, tomatoes, and onions, it's superb.

And when you're making centerpiece arrangements, remember that a few lustrous eggplants can be a gorgeous addition.

PEPPERS, SWEET AND HOT

Our sweet pepper production used to vary so much from year to year we thought it was a matter of luck. Not any more — though we still know chilly nights could turn our robust heat-lovers into forlorn waifs. In the summer of 1986 we had pepper plants so loaded with big green bells we couldn't eat them fast enough. We left some on the plants to turn red (and to double their vitamin C content; peppers are richer in vitamin C than citrus). They produced steadily until frost.

That led to our current recipe for good pepper production during short summers: either start your own seed indoors about ten weeks before planting time, or buy transplants. Put some variety in your seed order — Golden Bells, Purple Belle Hybrid, and Sweet Chocolate, to name a few, are all as pretty as their names when arranged on hors d'oeuvre platters.

To keep your young plants from being set back, don't put peppers out until the soil is really warm. It ought to be up to sixty-five degrees, four inches down, at 8:00 A.M. To warm the soil, in about mid-May spread clear or black plastic over the parts of the garden where heat-loving crops will be growing. On planting day, set the young transplants in slits in the plastic. The advantages of black plastic over clear, at least in the North, are that it not only holds down weeds but — being dark — contributes extra heat to the soil-warming process.

On the other hand, I was interested to read that experiments done in Alabama, where summers are very hot, showed that brown plastic is preferred over either clear or black. Brown plastic warms soil in spring, but doesn't allow it to overheat on very hot days in summer. Don't use organic mulches like leaves or straw around pepper plants until after you're sure the soil is warm; those mulches just keep the sun and air from heating the earth.

Peppers appreciate nitrogen in reasonable quantity, and need magnesium for production. To get peppers off to a good start, even if your soil is rich in compost and aged manure, it may help to put a teaspoon of 5-10-10 fertilizer in each planting hole. About two or three weeks later, side-dress with compost or composted manure. At the same time, you can provide magnesium by mixing a tablespoon of Epsom salts in a gallon of water and spraying the plants with it. Or just sprinkle a handful of Epsom salts around each plant, about four inches from the stem, and water it in.

Once your plants are in a good, well-drained location, give them plenty of water. The inch a week that books recommend is an absolute minimum. Regular watering by drip or spray is vital to good production of these fruits. Some gardeners like to fertilize as they water, using weak manure tea or weak fish emulsion.

As peppers mature, be a bit careful when you pick them. We use to just twist each one off its stem, but after breaking a couple of plants I've become more cautious. Now I cut each ripe one off with a sharp knife.

Both sweet and hot peppers grow on such neat, immaculate-looking plants that gardeners with limited space can set peppers out amid the flower beds around the house. The baby peppers, looking like little Christmas tree decorations, as well as the shiny, full-sized globes, hold their own among the bright summer flowers.

There are lots of theories about why people like to eat hot peppers, and I'm not sure which of them to believe. I do know gardeners enjoy telling each other about the chili peppers they've grown and how they taste. They're proud of how their peppers scorch the throat, cause profuse sweating, make their eyes turn up in their sockets, and clear the entire upper respiratory tract at first swallow. Then they reach for the water bucket, smiling through the tears.

One theory claims that when hot peppers are eaten in summer, they cause the body to perspire and become cooler, and that's why people don't mind burning their mouths and throats. (I can think of less painful ways to break out in a perspiration in August, like weeding at high noon.)

Some scientifically inclined persons say the pain from eating superhot peppers is great enough to make the brain release endorphins, those mysterious substances that give a sense of euphoria to one who is suffering. Could be, I think, could be.

I've learned to enjoy a little pepper pungency myself, and even admit that beneath the bite of a chili there's an elusive, very special flavor, just as there is with very hot radishes. But without an operation to insulate my throat, I'm sure I'll never be able to eat the most pungent peppers. Whenever I cook with hot peppers, I don my kitchen gloves so my hands won't get burned, and for my own consumption, I remove the seeds before using the peppers. Most of the pungency, which comes from the compound capsaicin, lies in the seeds.

It was inevitable that Americans would start taking to bitingly hot foods — they were coming at us from two directions, both sources having superb cuisines. Many hot Thai, Indian, and Chinese dishes, and many more from Mexico and South America, have been clasped to the hearts — or should I say stomachs? — of American gourmets.

THE PERFECT PUMPKIN

Our family hasn't tried to set any gardening records. We don't look for cabbages as big as beach balls or zucchini as hefty as shillelaghs, we just want enough harvest to feed us. Let other gardeners seek immortality in the *Guinness Book of World Records*. We'll concentrate on how many beans there are to freeze for winter and whether the daylilies have recovered since the neighbor's dogs raced through the flower bed.

Something happened a few years ago, however, that *did* make us wonder if it wouldn't be fun some time to try to get a prize for the biggest pumpkin at the Champlain Valley Fair, and it all came about by accident. Apparently in the spring one of us must have dropped a pumpkin seed near the back of the house by mistake, and it grew. I saw the little vine struggling, and figured it wasn't in anyone's way, so I left it. Then one day I saw its broad leaves spreading across the lawn. I felt as Jack must have felt when his bean-stalk headed for the clouds. The vine was growing with such enthusiasm we couldn't bear to uproot it. We let it writhe about all over our hill, and by summer's end it produced the biggest pumpkins we'd ever had. It didn't take us long to realize why. The seed had rooted right next to the down-spout from the caves, so it was watered thoroughly every time there was any rain. The downspout was an ideal grow-ing spot from the pumpkin's point of view — though cer-tainly not from a landscaper's.

To get such big fruits in the garden, where they belong, is a lot more work. For a prizewinner, we'd choose a variety such as Big Max, Atlantic Giant, Big Moon, or Mammoth Gold; they have the genetic potential for giantism. Then we'd give the vines superb care. These plants have the insatiable thirst of a desert traveler; they also want rich, well-drained soil and regular side-dressing every few weeks. We'd weed aggressively, but with care, because the vines are shallow-rooted.

To get really huge pumpkins, experts let just *one* grow on each vine. For insurance, I'd be inclined to leave three or four until they're about as big as baseballs; then it should be safe to remove all but the one that's making the best growth. Periodically we'd pinch off the fuzzy growing ends of the vine so it couldn't form any new fruits.

I've read that feeding milk to pumpkins makes them bigger. The idea is that you nip off the end of one of the stems and place the cut end in a dish of milk. Supposedly the vine will carry the milk to the pumpkin, which will fatten like a baby. But from what champion pumpkin growers tell me, I suspect this is just an old wives' tale.

After all our work we don't want to end up with a lopsided pumpkin that looks as if it's been in a prizefight. Big fruits flatten out along the bottom if left in the same position all season. We'll turn ours now and then so they will be symmetrical, but do it carefully — the stems damage very easily.

The safest way to harvest pumpkins is to cut them off the vine with a sharp knife or shears when they've turned orange; if the stem pulls away, it leaves a raw spot that invites decay.

To store extra pumpkins, cure them in a very warm, dry place for a week or ten days. A temperature between seventy-five and eighty degrees is ideal, if you can provide it. Then mix ten parts water to one part bleach and dip each fruit into it. This will kill any fungi and bacteria that may lurk invisibly on the skin. Store your pumpkins in a coolish (fifty- to sixty-degree), dry place. Don't use a root cellar, which is likely to be a bit damp. If you have an unheated attic, it should be excellent; some gardeners are able to make pumpkins last all winter in their attics.

Our house doesn't have an attic, so we store winter squash and pie pumpkins in a cool room. Come January I usually end up baking them and freezing the contents, because when even one shows signs of "going," I panic and am afraid for them all.

The big pumpkins grown for jack-o'-lanterns are edible, though not nearly as good as the smaller pumpkins bred for their superior taste; some people call them sugar pumpkins. If you raise pumpkins but not winter squash, you can use the pumpkins in squash recipes, they work just as well. You can also use these sweet pumpkins in sweet potato recipes. And, of course, there's no reason not to let the children carve some of the cooking pumpkins. Usually the vines are so prolific you can't possibly keep and use all the fruits, especially when they're only one of many vegetables in your garden.

Pumpkins don't have much protein, but they contain fifty-seven milligrams of calcium per cupful and are extremely rich in vitamin A — more so than winter squash.

They also have fewer calories than winter squash. Somehow I thought they'd be just alike, they seem so closely related. But one cup of cooked pumpkin contains just 75 calories, while a cup of winter squash has 130 calories. Of course if you add sugar to the pumpkin and use it in pie, you've changed the whole ball game. But pumpkin is delicious in soups, too, and you do *not* have to use heavy cream as most recipes recommend. If you start with a homemade, tasty chicken broth and use just a little white wine, you can make a yummy cream soup with skim milk. I know — I've done it.

Baskets of bright sugar pumpkins promise many delicious meals long after the garden is snow-covered; and a few huge pumpkins are a conversation piece in the neighborhood, a wonderful gift for youngsters, and, we trust, too awkward for vandals to carry off. The real giants call for a wheelbarrow or large cart. Maybe this year we *shall* take our biggest pumpkin to the county fair. Think how lovely it would look with a blue ribbon hanging from its curved stem.

° 17 °

Onions
and Leeks

Without onions, I don't think I could cook. For soups, sand-wiches, casseroles, roasts, salads, everything but desserts, I depend on onions — or on garlic or shallots or leeks, their sisters under the skin. Onions aren't very nutritious, but by making other foods sparkle with flavor, they help us enjoy the most nutritious dishes.

People have been eating onions for thousands of years. In Egyptian tombs dating back to 3000 B.C. there are pictures of workers devouring the pearly vegetables. Onions were used in religious ceremonies and public festivals, as well as on the dinner table. Very early in the Christian era, histori-ans reported eating onions, both red and white, round and flat. Rome's early writer Pliny even mentions that the red ones had a milder flavor.

Onions are never backward about putting themselves for-ward, so to speak. They *look* modest, but one whiff gives them away. Without question, this pungent power had much to do with their being used in special ceremonies.

Onions are so easy to grow, just about every food garden has some. They do insist on an appropriate day length, though. Gardeners in the South buy short-day onions that start to bulb when days are twelve to fourteen hours long. Gardeners up North buy long-day onions that form bulbs when days last fourteen to sixteen hours.

Much of the onion grows above ground, with just the lowest portion and the stringy roots under the soil surface. Soil makeup is important. Onions do best in light soil; if yours is heavy, be sure to add lots of organic matter to improve its texture.

Onions like to eat. We plant ours in compost-rich soil, and give them a side-dressing when the green spears are four or five inches tall. We side-dress with our own manure-rich compost, but 10-10-10 fertilizer works well too. Use one pound for every twenty- to twenty-five-foot row, forking it in alongside where the plants are growing.

The most troublesome part of onion production is storage. After the tops fall over in the garden, spread the onions on screens if possible, so the air can dry them, out of direct sunlight. At my house we spread them on old sheets on the warm brick terrace. We move them into the garage each night so they won't be dampened by morning dew.

In a week or two they're dry, their outer skins crisp and papery. At that stage we either braid them or put them in mesh bags and hang them in a little-used, fairly cool room. (Ideal storage conditions are just above thirty-two degrees and 60 to 70 percent humidity.) They keep all winter. If by chance one seems to be darkening, I remove it and throw it away. Toward spring, if some begin to sprout green tops, I use them promptly in soups or salad. That's what's so nice about onions; they have as many lives as a cat, and can be used at any stage from birth to rebirth.

The leek is an elegant cousin of the onion. In Europe the

leek is so cheap and plentiful it's called "the poor man's asparagus," but it's unusual enough in the United States to be sold as a gourmet item at fancy prices.

Like the onion, the leek has a long history. Leeks have been cultivated for over four thousand years. The ancient Egyptians held the leek to be sacred. It was popular during the heyday of the Roman Empire, too. Tales are told of the emperor Nero, of Rome-burning fame, insisting on eating a bowl of leek soup every day because he believed leeks were good for the vocal cords and therefore would make his speeches more impressive.

However that may be, this handsome vegetable certainly makes many cooks' specialties more impressive. The delicate flavor of the white lower part of the stem is pleasant if leeks are simply steamed or creamed. Or they can be made into the famous leek-and-potato soup called vichyssoise, or used in salads, stews, other soups, or stir-fries.

Leeks have many other virtues that make them attractive to the home gardener: they're not appealing to insects (some gardeners even believe that if you interplant leeks with other vegetables, the leeks may ward off harmful insects). And leeks are so hardy that if you supply a very thick mulch of straw — say a foot deep over and around them — you should be able to harvest them fresh all winter. That makes this one more vegetable you don't have to haul in from the garden in the busy days of fall; and one you don't have to find space for in the freezer.

About the only drawback I can think of is that sometimes it's hard to get all the earthy grit out from among the tightly wrapped leek leaves. The trick is first to cut off all the upper green part. The lower, whitened part is the only part you eat, after all. Then grab your leek by its roots and plunge it up and down rapidly in a tub of water, to force the water into the sheath of curled leaves. Or do what I do — cut the leek lengthwise into four sections; then you can see exactly where the grit is and get it out. Leeks are so big I cut mine before using them anyhow, so quartering certainly does them no harm — and the inside leaf arrangement is one of the beauties of the natural world.

Any gardening book will tell you how easy it is to grow leeks. Just remember, they like a long growing season but don't mind frost.

You'll probably need to start them indoors; they're often the first sign of the gardening season, as they can be started in January or February, depending on where you live.

If you let this year's leeks live under cover of mulch until next year, you can start a permanent supply. Leeks are biennials, so though they're not good to eat the second year, they will flower and seed. Run your hands over the big seed heads from time to time to release the seeds. Those that fall in fertile soil will come up very early the following spring and you may have harvest-size leeks by midsummer. If you're aiming to raise leeks for bulbs, grow only one variety at a time — unless you have room to separate varieties by one hundred feet to assure that each variety will come true.

Leeks left to grow their second year will produce corms underground in moderate-temperature areas. Plant those, and you have more free leeks. Thus, with any luck, the first leeks you buy can become great-great-great-grandparents in your garden.

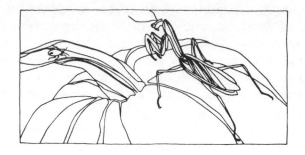

—— ○ 18 ○ ——

Helpful
Creatures

PRAYING MANTIS

The praying mantis is supposed to be the only insect that can look back over its shoulder. This is one of nature's little ironies, because it is other insects who had better look over their shoulders when any mantis is in the neighborhood.

Far from being religious, the prayer position is the mantis's waiting-to-pounce posture. The spelling of their name really ought to be p-r-e-y not p-r-a-y. Praying mantises' lovely mist-green color makes them hard to spot, and their delicate wings let them move freely among garden plants and shrubbery.

The mantis feeds only on living creatures and will attack anything smaller than itself, even another mantis. That's why the story arose that the female always eats the male after mating. That isn't actually part of the ritual, and some males depart safely, but there are times when a hungry female will indeed gobble up her mate.

The mantis has powerful legs with sharp spikes. Each leg is a double-edged saw ending in a sharply pointed hook. Guaranteed a sure grip by this combination of weapons, the mantis can consume her prey at leisure; her shackled prisoners are powerless.

Praying mantises can be a big help to the gardener, voraciously eating so-called bad bugs, and some good ones, too. Are there mantises in your garden? Their egg cases in the fall look like brown, curled leaves or one-and-a-half-inch ovals of sand-colored ocean foam attached to a twig, weed, or grass — almost anything as long as there is an uneven surface to which it can attach. To make the egg case, the female releases a golden substance and beats it into froth with two ladlelike structures at the back of her body. Even while releasing the foam and carefully building the nest, she ejects her eggs. In two minutes, the foam hardens like plastic, enclosing the eggs safely so they can overwinter.

Young mantises usually emerge on a bright, sunny day in June. The grubs are reddish yellow, wrapped in smooth protective covering. They quickly shake off these silky swaddling clothes and assume the adult shape except for the wings, which develop as they grow. Like the snake, the mantis discards its old coverings and grows new ones as it matures. Sometimes you see these empty shells hanging from twigs in the garden, like the ghosts of ancient mantises.

Some gardeners buy mantis egg cases to set in their gardens, hoping for help in pest control. This may or may not be helpful. Many report that they see the eggs hatch in spring but that the young mantises don't stick around. Remember, if a mantis can't find enough insects in your garden to appease her gluttony, she'll go foraging.

This is true of any of the helpful insects that gardeners sometimes order by mail. If you cage them, they can't do their job, and if you don't, they will go to the dining area of their choice. You can only hope this will be in your garden. They may stay with you until they've cleaned things up in your garden, then move on. They won't stick around and wait for new prey to appear; apart from mating, eating is the whole object and consuming passion of their lives.

EARTHWORMS

Giant cobras and fat boa constrictors are fascinating creatures. Yet to me, they are no more astonishing than the earthworm, and a good deal less useful.

Earthworms aerate the soil. They wiggle through it when it's loose and crumbly like a fresh muffin; they eat their way through when it's fairly compact. They open up spaces that let moisture and air reach your plant roots. Soil goes into a worm at one end and comes out, much improved, at the other. Then it's called worm castings.

Earthworms pass their weight in castings daily. Whatever nutrients the worms don't need are available to plants in the castings; and they're in a form readily absorbed by plant roots. Worms even pull leaf scraps and other organic material down into their burrows. They eat what they need and leave the rest to enrich the soil. Charles Darwin estimated that an acre of good soil might contain sixty-three thousand earthworms. Sixty-three thousand worms can deposit eighteen *tons* of castings each year. That's two inches of new topsoil every decade.

Even dead, the worms are useful. As their bodies decompose, 70 percent of the nitrogen trapped in their tissues is released.

Many gardeners believe that if they accidentally cut a

worm in half when spading the garden, it doesn't matter. "It'll make two worms," they say. In fact, if the worm happens to be cut in the right place, it may regrow some parts and become one whole worm; but it won't make two. The head end, if left with enough segments, can regenerate. A nightcrawler can replace 2 or 3 body segments of its 150; red wigglers can replace 8. So a head section may be able to grow a new tail, but the cut-off tail section will die.

Earthworms breathe through their skin. If brought to the surface and left in the sun, they shrivel and die. You can help them in summer by watering during dry spells. Use mulches to keep the soil cool and moist. In the cool dampness of fall, earthworms are at their most active stage: their eggs hatch, and young worms mature and leave their burrows to mate. We wish them every success.

LADYBUGS

"Ladybird, ladybird, fly away home" — my home, *please!* For all the garden bugs that cause me trouble, it's always such a joy to find an insect that's not only a menace to some of the bad bugs in the garden but that's attractive, too. Did you know that ladybugs can gulp down fifty aphids a day, or that their larvae can eat forty in one hour? I'm astounded by their voracious appetites. Go to it, ladies.

Ladybugs, alias ladybird beetles, got their complimentary name in the Middle Ages, when European farmers, grateful for their help in protecting their vineyards, dedicated all ladybugs to "Our Lady," the Virgin Mary.

Ladybugs are brightly colored and can give off an unpleasant odor (though it's not always perceptible to the human sense of smell), possibly to warn off birds and other predators. A ladybug larva is an even better predator than its parents, and doesn't have their misleadingly comfortable, unthreatening appearance. Ladybug larvae *look* like predators; their flat, dark gray bodies have blue or orange spots and taper to the tail. Though we commonly think of ladybugs as aphid controls, they also prey on root worms, weevils, chinch bugs, and Colorado potato beetles.

We had no ladybugs in this country until cottony cushion scale threatened the citrus groves in California, late in the last century. The citrus industry faced extinction until a USDA entomologist in Australia found ladybugs feeding on the scale. The United States imported ladybugs by the hundreds of thousands, and the crisis ended in two years.

Some ladybugs winter over in garden plants and weeds. Other types head for cold areas, such as the Western highlands. This time out for chilling is called diapause. Once when my family visited Kitt Peak Observatory in Arizona, we stopped near the top to stare and wonder at the pillow-sized gathering of ladybugs on a walkway railing. They were in diapause, and we were so captivated we darn near joined them.

Forest rangers in the Rocky Mountains scoop up huge masses of these wintering ladybugs in sacks and put them in cold storage. Next spring they're released to orchards and fields. Managers of insect farms also raise ladybugs for sale to farmers and gardeners. Buying ladybugs isn't likely to be a reliable pest control for gardeners, however. For one thing, our gardens are usually small, and as soon as the pest insects are gone, the ladybugs fly off to seek a more consistent food source. Also, the little beetles are programmed, so to speak, to disperse after diapause, so even with ample prey available they scatter quickly; some experts feel it's a waste of money to buy them.

However, if you are really badly pestered by aphids, scales, spider mites, or other tiny pests, and want to try ladybugs, proceed with care. First ask the seller which species prefers the pest that's most bothersome to you, so you're sure of getting the right ladies. When they arrive, release them late in the evening in an area with damp mulch for shelter, so they'll stick around all night and seek a food source in your garden. If they arrive before you're quite ready to release them, put the package in the refrigerator for a while. The insects will continue diapause there for several weeks if need be.

In watching ladybugs in the garden, don't confuse them with the Mexican bean beetles, which are horrid pests. The bean beetle has sixteen spots on its back, none on its thorax, and a slightly fuzzy coat; ladybugs have twelve or fewer spots and smooth coats.

Ladybugs work hard for us in the garden, and there's no charge. Whoever taught youngsters to chant "Ladybird, ladybird, fly away home" was definitely not a gardener.

HONEYBEES

Gardeners would be playing a losing game if it were not for bees. Yet few of us are beekeepers; we rely on wild bees, or bees from neighbors' hives, to pollinate our melons, cucumbers, squashes, and various fruit crops.

Gardeners with fruit trees are the most bee-dependent. Researchers have found that fruit trees may need as many as one bee for every hundred blossoms to get good crop pollination. Most orchardists keep beehives. Those of us with just a few trees, who may not keep bees, need to know how to persuade them to visit.

So it's helpful to know a little about them — how to attract them to the garden, how to avoid stings, and what to do if you happen to be stung.

Bees are attracted to water. Just setting a water-filled pie plate atop a post in the garden can be a good lure. They don't like wet blooms, though, so overhead sprinkling at blossom time can reduce their activity.

Mass plantings attract bees. A bee in search of pollen and nectar doesn't want to have to fly up and down six different aisles in your garden-supermarket to locate occasional cucumber blossoms. It wants lots of those big yellow blooms in one area, so it can do its gathering efficiently.

Fortunately, honeybees are willing to do some window shopping. While a foraging bee is working on the lima beans, it may just mosey over to the cukes or melons or tomatoes to be sure it isn't missing anything; and of course it will pollinate some blooms in the process. Tomatoes are among the crops that don't need bees to pollinate them; they self-pollinate as wind or insects jostle the blossoms, but it's been found that tomato plants give significantly heavier yields when bees visit their blossoms. It helps to have those bees shaking the flowers as they use them for landing pads.

A large colony of honeybees will collect as much as seventy-five pounds of pollen in one season. That's a lot of shopping trips. Since we don't let some of our vegetable crops bloom, it helps to provide some heavy-flowering ornamentals that bees like. Lavish plantings of asters, cleome, lythrum, butterfly weed, petunias, and other flowers around the garden perimeter won't take up food-growing space and will please bees. They also love many herbs that are useful and handsome as border plantings. The trick that takes some forethought is choosing flowers and herbs that bloom at the same time the bee-dependent crop blooms. A variety of honeybee favorites, giving a constant succession of bloom all summer, is the easiest way to go.

Now as to bee stings. First, remember the bee is tending strictly to business and not looking for people to sting. It will sting only if you get in the way. To avoid stings, wear whites and pastel colors when you're in the garden, rather than very bright or dark things. Never wear perfume; you don't want to be mistaken for flowers. Don't wave your arms and try to chase bees that are at work in the garden; you'll just get them all excited. Leave them alone and they'll go home, carrying the pollen behind them.

Some folks, of course, react severely to bee stings and don't want to take any chance of encountering bees whatsoever. For them a sting can mean an emergency trip to the hospital — or at the least, a treatment with an antihistamine or an injection available by special prescription. For the rest of you, if a sting happens, don't pull the stinger out with tweezers, you'll just squeeze more venom into the wound. Scrape the stinger off with the back of a knife or with your fingernail, then apply baking soda paste and ice to help relieve the pain. You might even take a moment to feel sorry for the honeybee; it was frightened into stinging you, and in losing its stinger it perished. After all, it was only trying to help.

——— ∘ 19 ∘ ———

Pesticides: Natural Is
Not Always Safe

Supermarket foods whose labels proclaim they contain "one hundred percent natural ingredients" attract buyers. Shoppers seem to believe that any food made without chemical additives must be good for us. Yet salt, sugar, and fats are all natural, and certainly not good for us, at least in large quantities. So "natural" doesn't mean "safe" — after all, poison ivy's natural, too.

Similarly, gardeners may forget that natural pest and disease controls can be dangerous. There are three natural plant poisons commonly used in this country: pyrethrum, rotenone, and nicotine. Pyrethrum comes from the flowers of certain chrysanthemums; rotenone comes from roots of various species of tropical legumes like *Derris elliptica* and *Lonchocarpus*; and nicotine, of course, comes from the debris left after tobacco production. Each of these poisons must actually touch the insect in order to kill it.

Pyrethrum works fast, but doesn't stay in the environment long. It kills flying insects — not only flies and mosquitoes, but also wasps (some of which are garden helpers) and bees. Use it at dusk when these buzzing insects have returned to their hives. You can spray with pyrethrum up to a day or two before harvesting your vegetables. Persons with allergies are especially sensitive to pyrethrum and should wear protective clothing if they use pyrethrum sprays.

Rotenone, like pyrethrum, disappears within a few days from the environment. Though natural, both are still poisons; if they weren't, they wouldn't kill pests. They can be dangerous if used improperly. If you do use them, wear a surgical or dust mask when applying; inhaling either rotenone or pyrethrum can cause irritation of the nose, throat, or lungs.

Nicotine is more dangerous than either rotenone or pyrethrum. Gardeners are usually advised to use only three teaspoons of the normal nicotine sulfate solution to a gallon of water, which gives you an idea of how strong the stuff is. It can cause nausea, abdominal pain, vomiting, diarrhea, mental confusion, and weakness. It can even be absorbed through the skin, so it requires extremely careful handling. Never, never spray it on any part of a plant that will be eaten. Its primary use is against aphids. Heck, we can wash aphids off with a hose or soap spray; or let the ladybugs have them for dinner. So: of the three "natural" plant-derived controls mentioned, I would suggest using only rotenone and pyrethrum, *if* you need them. Forget nicotine.

A natural insecticide that is completely safe is *Bacillus thuringiensis* or Bt, a bacterium. When you spray plants with this, caterpillars (anything from cabbage loopers to the big tomato hornworms) ingest the spores. The spores grow inside them and within two hours the worms stop eating; in a couple of days they die. You can wash and eat Bt-sprayed plants at any time.

Before investing in any of these insecticides try hand-picking, then resort to simple soap sprays. You don't need an elaborate arsenal to protect a small plot. That's one of the reasons home gardeners are good for the environment — they can produce food without adding poisons to air or earth.

∘ 20 ∘

Perennial
Greats

IRISES

Midsummer is merely maintenance time in the flower garden, and a good thing too, as the food gardens keep us pretty
busy. It's a treat to be able to gather a flower bouquet to
take into the house after weeding the onions for an hour
and harvesting some greens for supper. The one flower that
calls for some real work at this time is the iris, and we've
lots of them around our house. The ideal time to divide and
plant irises is after they finish flowering. Luckily, we don't
have to do it every year; our irises consider themselves
lucky if we manage it once in five to eight years, by which
time their roots are so entangled with grass and weed roots
it's a major chore. Don't imitate us. Divide your irises every
three to five years if at all possible.

Aptly named after the goddess of the rainbow, irises come in just about all colors. The tall German bearded irises are probably the most common in gardens, but there are many other species and hybrids to choose from. All have the same flower structure: six petals, three upright ones known as standards and three hanging down, called falls. Tall bearded irises and some of the dwarf species have a fuzzy line or "beard" down the center of each fall. The little crested iris has a small raised ridge instead of a beard, and the beardless irises, like the Siberian and Japanese types, have smooth petals and thin, grasslike leaves.

Bearded irises grow from rhizomes, thick underground stems like flattened bulbs. They need well-drained soil with a pH near neutral and full sun to do their best. Japanese and Siberian irises have fibrous root systems; they like moist, slightly acid soil and are more tolerant of shade. The Japanese irises are fussier than the Siberian, and may need winter protection in a cold climate.

Midsummer to late summer is the time to plant new iris rhizomes or to divide established clumps of bearded irises. Plant them by the end of August so they'll have time to get established before winter; though I must say, our experience is that the iris is a survival expert. When dividing bearded irises, cut the leaves back to about a third of their height and divide the rhizomes with a sharp knife. Be sure each division has at least one growing point, or fan of leaves, some well-developed roots, and a few inches of healthy rhizome.

Set the plants out in groups of three or four, to get a good color effect, and put the rhizomes about six or seven inches apart. Plant bearded irises with the roots in the ground, but the top of the rhizome visible; sun and air on the top of the rhizome discourage iris borers that can quickly destroy plants.

The best time to divide or plant beardless Siberian or Japanese irises is spring. Dividing the fibrous clump of beardless iris rhizomes can be tough; you may need a sharp spade. Cut vigorous outer sections of the clump of roots into chunks about five inches across, and discard the weak center part.

Few flowers are as rewarding as irises, to my mind. The brilliance of their color, the beauty of their foliage, the hardiness of at least the bearded ones, make them the gardener's friend. Their broad, sharpened spears of green add beauty to the springtime long before the gorgeous blooms appear. I happen to think an iris is every bit as lovely as the most exotic orchid, and a good deal easier to grow.

DAYLILIES

I love daylilies. And to think my husband had to introduce me to their virtues — a husband who, before he got daylily mania, claimed there was no point in raising anything we couldn't eat. Actually daylilies *are* edible; the blossoms are good dipped in batter and fried, and the little bumps on the roots, carefully peeled, are deliciously crisp in salads.

Our main reason for favoring these jewel-like blossoms is that they make no demands on us. Put them in halfway decent soil, in either full sun or partial shade, and they'll produce. Though each daylily bloom lives up to its name by opening for only a single day, each plant produces so many flowers that they provide constant beauty.

Since 1930, breeders in this country have been turning out new daylily varieties with unprecedented inventiveness. The gardener's biggest challenge may be choosing which to buy.

The first daylilies grown by American gardeners were native to Asia. Among these were the yellow lemon daylily and the orange tawny daylily brought to the United States by European settlers; the so-called "wild" orange daylilies we see growing by roadsides are in fact just escapees from the early gardens. In the late 1930s, a plant-collecting expedition in Asia sent the New York Botanical Garden a red-flowered variant of the tawny daylily. Dr. Arlo B. Stout, the granddaddy of daylily breeders here, used that red daylily to breed peach, pink, red, and wine-colored varieties.

Daylilies aren't really lilies. They belong to the genus *Hemerocallis*, a name derived from two Greek words. *Hemera* means day and *kallos* means beauty; the botanists who named these flowers surely had poetry in their souls.

Many daylily varieties flower during the heat of summer when few other perennials are in bloom. They're an excellent choice for preventing erosion on a steep slope; that's one of the ways we use them at our house. Their roots keep the soil anchored, and established clumps can grow so thickly, weeds don't have a chance. (Except, let me say, for burdock, which seems to enjoy daylily companionship and drives me crazy.)

I suppose there must be some pests or diseases that attack daylilies, but we've never encountered any. I've read that daylily breeders, in their quest to produce ever more spectacular flowers, have let some disease- and pest-resistant characteristics be lost in the newest hybrids. But at home we stick with the older, tried and true beauties, usually more moderately priced, so we've yet to have a problem.

You can leave daylilies alone almost forever and they will still look good, I think; but they will be more vigorous if divided every four or five years. If you divide your daylily clumps, do it in early spring so plants have a chance to make themselves at home before winter comes. Make sure each division has plenty of roots and at least two clumps of leaves. Set divisions about two feet apart with the crown of the plant an inch below the soil, water well, and jump back. The eager-to-grow daylily will do the rest. When we divide we end up with — what else? — lots more daylilies — more than enough to put in new places on our own land, and some to give to friends.

—— ∘ 21 ∘ ——

The Scented Garden

OF SCENTS AND SPIRITS

Amid all the unusual botanical research going on these days, I wonder whether anyone has checked the effect of plants' scents on human feelings? Certainly earlier science-minded persons considered it. Roman naturalist Pliny the Elder, speaking of mint, pointed out that "the very smell alone recovers and refreshes our spirits." Perhaps that's one reason mint juleps are so popular in the South, especially on Kentucky Derby day. Maybe it isn't just the bourbon that consoles losers and helps winners celebrate; maybe it's also the pungent, woodsy, outdoorsy smell of the fresh chopped mint garnishing their glasses.

The sixteenth-century herbalist John Gerard claimed that sniffing basil "taketh away melancholy and maketh a man merry and glad." And other herbalists believed that "the scent of wild thyme raises the spirits and strengthens the vital energies." I don't know about my vital energies, but I do know that I, and everyone else in my household, love to walk on the wild thyme that spreads alongside our garden steps. It *does* refresh our spirits, and we never leave the spot without picking a sprig to sniff as we climb the hill.

In recent years, some well-known gardeners have remarked on the power of garden aromas. Writer Louise Beebe Wilder said she found the smell of clove pinks instantly invigorating, and inhaling the scent of old-fashioned roses calming and soothing. For me, the aroma of lavender conjures pictures of home and hearth and puts me in a quiet, nostalgic mood, while for some reason the smell of violets makes me hungry. I nearly always eat a few blossoms on the spot; they're suprisingly sweet.

Scents and flavors go together. I think that's why herbs do such wonderful things for some dishes. I never, never cook chicken without adding anywhere from a dash to a small handful of marjoram (depending on how much chicken I have). I know many cooks prefer sage with chicken, but I think marjoram heightens the natural flavor of the meat. Sprinkle a bit of marjoram on your next chicken salad or cup of chicken soup, and see if you don't agree. That isn't to say I don't like sage in chicken or turkey stuffing; I do. That's one cooking tradition I don't break.

I do break one of the lamb traditions, though. To me, mint overpowers the delicate lamb flavor. Instead I use rosemary, lots of it. If you grow a rosemary bush, you'll find just rubbing your hand over the leaves and inhaling deeply gives you a healthy, invigorated feeling. The dried leaves worked into lamb patties recall that feeling for you.

Tarragon's aroma invites culinary experiments. Tarragon is great with eggs. Melt a little butter in a small baking dish, break an egg into it, stir in some chopped fresh tarragon and a little cream, then bake for just four or five minutes. Or add fresh tarragon to omelets, stuffed hard-boiled eggs, or even plain old scrambled eggs.

I believe every scent-and-flavor garden should have some sweet woodruff. Its aroma is dizzyingly magical — elegant, delicious, unforgettable. For your own May wine, try crushing some leaves in white wine for a few hours, then strain them out, chill the wine and taste. Aaaaaah.

GERANIUMS

For an indoor scented garden, get acquainted with scented geraniums. I know gardeners whose hobby is collecting geranium varieties, and the list seems endless — apple, ginger, cinnamon, lemon, rose, even nutmeg and pepper. A shelf of scented geranium plants is like a living spice rack. In addition to their aroma, many of the scented geraniums have interesting foliage. Several have almost ferny leaves. Others have deeply lobed leaves, others variegated leaves, and some have silvery gray foliage. I think all of these are as attractive to the eye as to the nose.

My introduction to scented geraniums came at a friend's house. On her sunny kitchen windowsill sat a plant with attractive, finely cut foliage. I examined it closely, and as I looked, I absent-mindedly ran my hand over the lacy leaves. At once I was enveloped by the most delectable, lemony scent. It turns out I was stroking the scented geranium *Pelargonium radens* 'Doctor Livingston'. When its leaves are gently pressed, it fills the room with a pungent, fruity fragrance.

Scented geraniums, native to southern Africa, were first brought to Europe in the seventeenth century. Their heyday was in the Victorian era, when they were used to freshen the air in the closed-up "company parlor."

Like all geraniums, the scented species will bloom indoors in a sunny spot, although the flowers don't rival those of their showy common geranium counterparts. If you spend most of your summer days outdoors, put the scented plants out too. That's bound to bring a bloom out of them.

But what you really care about are those fruity, spicy leaves, so don't be fussy about lighting as long as the plants don't get spindly. The plants do best if you let them dry out slightly between waterings — not so dry that the leaves yellow through, however. Apply any basic house-plant fertilizer when the plants are growing actively in spring and again in fall to give them a boost. They're easy to propagate from cuttings, and there isn't a better gift to party hosts than one of these deliciously fragrant home-grown plants.

You can dry the leaves and use them in potpourri to scent every room in the house. You can even cook with them. Place a few leaves in the bottom of the pan next time you bake a cake. (Be sure the leaves you use have never been treated with pesticide.) Pour the batter on top and the fragrance and flavor of the leaves will subtly permeate the dessert. When the cake is done, peel off the leaves and discard them. When your family asks you what that delicious dessert flavor is, do you dare say, "geranium"?

OLD ROSES

Today there's renewed interest in the old rose varieties. Some of these old-fashioned beauties don't go on flowering throughout the season, but some do; and nearly all have lovely blossoms and a delicious scent. Many are cold-hardier than their modern cousins, and just about all of them grow well without imperiously demanding special care, as the beautiful but bossy tea roses do.

I've been looking into some of the choices, starting with *Rosa gallica*, considered the granddaddy of garden roses. It hybridizes readily with other roses. Such species as the alba, the autumn damask, and the centifolia, or cabbage rose, may all have risen from crosses with gallicas. Then in the late 1700s, much more delicate and tender roses were brought to Europe from China. When crossed with gallica roses, these produced many new species including, ultimately, our hybrid tea roses.

Gallicas are shrublike plants that reach three to four feet tall with blossoms in shades of red or purple. Some have spotted, striped, or mottled flowers. These ancient roses have a strong tendency to produce sports or mutations on parts of the plant, so some day you may be surprised to see a new combination of colors or patterns on some branches. Gallicas are hardy to USDA Zone 4. One of the oldest is *R. gallica* 'Officinalis', the apothecary rose. It has light crimson, semidouble blossoms that smell like heaven.

The alba roses are taller than gallicas, some reaching eight feet, with small fragrant flowers in clusters. They flower early, resist disease, and are winter-hardy and fragrant.

The old-fashioned Bourbon roses are named for the Isle of Bourbon, off the coast of Madagascar, where they were first discovered. Most have the repeat-flowering habit, but as tender China roses are in their ancestry, they're hardy only to Zone 6.

One group of old-fashioned roses that I really appreciate in my Vermont garden are the rugosas. Very winter-hardy, disease-resistant, and fragrant, they flower repeatedly.

For a rose with the romance of the English countryside, mentioned in many British novels, try the eglantine or sweetbrier rose (*R. eglanteria*). It's hardy to Zone 3.

A neighbor who has some eglantines says that so far they've survived two winters, though hers haven't flowered yet. Eglantines are tall and supposed to be climbers. If my neighbor's roses show that tendency, I might try some on a trellis against our garage.

The only caution I can think of in connection with old roses is that they're addictive. Once you discover their simple charm in a bush or two, you'll find you want more. Even the names of these old-fashioned beauties in the catalogs are seductive: 'Boule de Neige', 'Reine des Violettes', *R. centifolia* 'Blanche Fleur'. Before we know it, you and I may both find we've added half a dozen old-rose varieties to our gardens.

LILACS

Lilacs make me sneeze. So do a lot of things, and I try to avoid most of them. But I don't try to avoid lilacs. The treat of inhaling their heady fragrance is well worth the price of a few sneezes.

Lilac bushes are so generous. Each plant grows gnarled-looking branches that make the bare shrub appear to have been designed for a fairy tale landscape peopled by leprechauns and satyrs. In May, lilacs explode with a lavish display of the flowers that gave the color lilac its name. When lilacs are at their height, they make our towns appear dressed to receive royalty. Rows of tall old lilacs lifting their blooms to the sun in a churchyard or park are impressive; a single bush standing by the garden gate gives a yard a homelike and inviting air.

Lilacs seem old-fashioned and inspire a sense of nostalgia. Our great-grandmothers had lilac bushes, just as we do. They're easy to grow and care for, and adaptable to a wide range of landscapes and growing conditions.

Lilacs are top-heavy, so you can use them in special ways in the landscape. Common lilacs will grow to a height of twelve to sixteen feet, and as the foliage starts high on the plants, you can grow flowers under them for full-season color.

Plant lilac bushes in well-drained soil and full sun in early spring. As they grow, prune away the lower root suckers to make the upper bloom more dramatic. New lilac hybrids have sterile seeds, so you don't need to remove spent flower heads; but with old varieties, the dedicated gardener will cut off dead blooms when they fade because seed formation takes energy away from the development of new flower buds. As your lilac grows, you may need a ladder for this job, though you may be able to bend the branches down within reach. To keep this shrub vigorous, prune out dead wood to the ground and remove one-quarter to one-third of the old wood every three to five years.

Most varieties we see today are derived from hybrids of common lilacs (*Syringa vulgaris*), developed at the turn of the century by a French nurseryman, Victor Lemoine. One scaled-down version is the Japanese tree lilac (*S. reticulata*). It makes a small compact tree and bears handsome ivory-colored blooms in June. The cultivar 'Ivory Silk' is shrublike and has superior bloom and foliage. Chinese (*S. × chinensis*) and Persian (*S. × persica*) hybrids, which come in a variety of colors — white to pale lavender to deep purple — bear greater masses of bloom than common lilacs.

Chinese and Persian varieties are smaller than the common variety, so they may save you some pruning work. They stay fairly bushy at the base and are among the cultivars handy for people with one-story houses, who don't want lilac bushes that grow higher than the roof.

---° 22 °---

Gardening
as Therapy

It was one of those days. The morning was sunny and
breezy, so by nine o'clock my wash was on the line, and
some plums, with a guesser's amount of sugar, were bub-
bling on the stove, turning themselves into jam.

I went to the typewriter, because for once I had an idea.
No need to wait and see what I wrote to find what I thought,
as sometimes happens.

The phone rang . . . the dentist's office. "Where are you?
You had an eight-thirty appointment." Too late. Feeling
horribly apologetic and guilty, I wrote down the new appointment time in three separate places.

A horrified glance out the window on the way back to the
typewriter revealed that one long clothesline had broken,
and sheets were billowing along the ground and catching on
the thorny multiflora roses.

By the time the sheets were pulled free and rewashed, the line fixed, and everything rehung, quite a few of the plums had grimly fastened themselves to the bottom of the pot and burned. Furiously I scooped them into the garbage (even the unstuck ones had absorbed the burnt taste), then set the scraped pot to soak with some soda and water. By this time my big idea had fled, and the typewriter just sat there, blank and waiting.

Forget it. When three things go wrong by midmorning, there's only one thing to do. Head for the garden. The beans needed weeding. Great: something to work out my resentments on. I knelt and started; the lamb's-quarters and pigweed pulled out easily, so I ripped them out angrily, in big handfuls. That felt good. After a few minutes I was enjoying the comforting feel of the soft, warm earth. I noticed the tiny beans were coming along just as they should, in elegant clusters hanging straight down.

As the weed heap grew and the row of handsome, weed-free plants extended behind me, I realized I wasn't frowning anymore; actually, I was smiling.

Two rows took an hour. The rich earth looked as inviting as heaped chocolate around the leafy green plants. Lugging baskets of weeds to the compost pile, downhill, then back up, made a nice healthy stretch after kneeling for so long. Then I carried armloads of *Boston Globe*s and *Wall Street Journal*s to the bean rows and laid them down in thick, overlapped mats on both sides of the rows. We even had some hay on hand to cover them. Now the bean rows were ready to have their picture taken.

The thick mulch along the row felt springy underfoot as I walked over to the carrots. I brushed my hands across their tops — there's a sensuous feel to a thick mass of feathery carrot greens. Pulling a couple of young ones, I rubbed them on my jeans and ate them. Crisp, slightly cool, sweet — my, they tasted good. As I chewed, my muscles relaxed and I reveled in the feel of the warm sun on my back. I listened a moment to a pair of robins arguing, then headed to the house.

Back to the typewriter. This time the words came readily. As I started striking the keys I realized I was grinning idiotically to myself.

Is gardening therapeutic? You bet it is.

————○ *23* ○————

Critter Control

MIDNIGHT RAIDERS

Woodchucks are as fond of the fruits of our garden as we are, and are even better at harvesting them. I've found these fat rodents will give everything but onions a taste — and I'm sure that out there somewhere is a woodchuck that likes onions in its salads.

Woodchucks have several aliases: groundhogs, whistle pigs (for the piercing sound they make when alarmed), and, scientifically, *Marmota monax*. They roam just about everywhere east of the central Great Plains and north of the Gulf States, and even in a few isolated pockets in the Western states. It's been estimated there's a woodchuck for every five to ten acres in the Northeast. That works out to a lot of woodchucks — and we have no one to blame but ourselves. Before Europeans settled here, most woodchucks lived in beaver meadows and natural clearings. As people cleared the forests, the woodchucks happily moved out to the grassy meadows. At the same time, the number of predators that fed on woodchucks — bears, wolves, mountain lions, and fishers — was reduced. All this made life easier for woodchucks and harder for gardeners.

Infuriating as they can be, woodchucks are interesting creatures. Some nongardeners actually find them cute. They're the largest wild animals commonly seen gorging themselves in our gardens. Old males often weigh as much as fifteen pounds; the one that used to think our vegetable garden was his pantry looked as if he weighed twenty or more.

Woodchucks are brazen. Once when I got up early to look over the garden, I saw, at the end of a row of decimated bean plants, a fat woodchuck sleeping off his meal. I shouted at him; he slept on. I clapped my hands loudly; he never stirred. Finally I poked him gently with a stick. He opened his eyes, stretched, gave me an insolent look, and waddled off — slowly.

One woodchuck control can be planting nasturtiums around the edge of the garden; I've never tried it, but I've heard woodchucks dislike nasturtium foliage. You can also try putting a small can of gasoline a short distance from the opening of the woodchuck's burrow. Supposedly the fumes fill the burrow and the chuck moves to better-smelling quarters.

We've heard from gardeners who save the family urine and pour it around the edge of the garden to keep woodchucks away. They report it works at least some of the time.

Gardens with persistent woodchuck problems may need fencing at least three feet high, with another foot underground to keep the chucks from tunneling under. Bend the underground piece so part of it sticks straight down and part is parallel to the soil surface; that should stop any tunnelers.

Humane traps are a lot better than any other means I can think of for gardeners and householders to get rid of beasties who think your world is their larder.

My family has caught a few critters in these traps, though not without some pretty lively discussions about who was in charge and how to deal with the furry prisoners. The first time we set a trap out for a woodchuck she ate our peanut butter and spinach bait and backed right out; she was so fat the trap door wouldn't close over her rear end. We borrowed a bigger trap. We trucked the pudgy glutton across a nearby river and released her outside town. You must lug woodchucks far away — at least five miles — or you may find a very physically fit woodchuck chomping your beans after it's walked all the way back to your garden. And of course, you *don't* want to dump chucks near anybody else's garden.

Our woodchuck had babies, and we felt the family should be together. We certainly didn't want two youngsters going through their adolescence on our garden vegetables. We caught them, one at a time, on two successive days, each time covering the trap with a rug to stop the young one from shrieking that the world was coming to an end. We released the offspring where we had released their fat parent, and assume that the family reunited quickly.

Besides wrestling with woodchucks, we've had close encounters with skunks. The humane traps that cage the animals so you can release them elsewhere are all very well; but in the case of a skunk, when the trap works, what you have is a skunk that you have to deal with.

"Just drive a few miles into the country and release it," say the neighbors who don't have a skunk-filled trap.

Getting a skunk *into* a trap is easy. You set the trap at night with a bait of tuna fish; skunks love it. So there is your animal, full of tuna fish and sitting in the trap. What next? Eau do sconque is hardly your choice for a car spray, but how can you avoid it?

You and the skunk must keep calm (everyone's advice for

everyone else's crisis). To keep the skunk calm, you cover the trap with a dark tarp or blanket you can live without. Tiptoe to the cage in the early morning (the skunk feeds at night) and quietly lower the blanket over it.

Then go away and let the animal adjust to what must seem to him like the shortest day on record. If the skunk is calm, you're calm, so the first part of the instruction has been followed. Next, carry the covered cage to the car or pickup truck. The latter is best, if you have one or can borrow one. But if you must use the family car, better put the trap on the roof. Set the trap on a piece of plywood to make it easier to lift and carry, and lash it to the cartop with the cage cover well tucked in. (In fact, it's easier to set the trap atop the plywood when you first set it out.)

Drive to a wooded spot or lonely field somewhere outside town, put the cage down with the exit door away from you, lift the cover and the door, and the skunk will scuttle off without a backward glance. He's had all the confusion he wants from you, thank you very much.

(It should be noted that in some municipalities it's against the law to deport trapped animals: they must be turned over to a vet, animal shelter, humane society, or other appropriate organization.)

I understand there are also mouse-sized catch-and-release traps. I have no experience with these — we've always had a cat or a dog. I'm not sure I have any soft spot for mice, so I'd be inclined to stick with the old-fashioned spring trap. Besides, where would you go to release a house mouse?

CROWS

The *World Book Encyclopedia* calls the common crow "a very intelligent bird." That's true enough — what I resent is that they're so much smarter than we are. They're supposed to be only *birds*, for heaven's sake. We can cover our strawberry beds with black mesh that terrifies all other birds, who fear imprisonment. Not the crows. They fly down and examine the nets with their beady little eyes, strutting stiffly about on their very strong crows' feet. As soon as the birds spot an overlap where pieces of netting meet, they step in with those well-adapted feet and use their long, sharp bills to tug the nets back. Then they go for the strawberries, taking a peck or two out of all the biggest and reddest ones. When they're full, they call in the rest of the family for a taste.

Perhaps the prize statement (or rather, understatement of the century) in my encyclopedia is: "The crow does not have a musical voice." Good *grief*. Have you heard a dozen crows screeching and hollering away in the trees at 4:30 of a summer morning? Saying their voices aren't musical is like saying the North Star isn't nearby. A crow's caw is the harshest, loudest, most grating, most infuriating sound any gardener is ever subjected to.

And crows, like children, use their powerful voices for *all* messages. If Papa crow wants to tell his wife and kids he's found some freshly planted corn and there's enough for all, does he fly over to grate out the message in his normal, hoarse, ten-decibel voice? Don't be ridiculous. He screeches from wherever he happens to be, and even if they're half a mile away, his family will hear that file-rough, ear-shattering sound. So will sleeping children, hitherto relaxed and quiet dogs, and persons struggling to have a conversation in the bean patch.

The encyclopedia does point out that crows will eat corn as soon as it's visible after planting and will consume other birds' eggs and infants. But the book seems to encourage its young readers to look on the bright side by saying that crows help us by eating insects and that "they make good pets if obtained when young; sometimes their owners can teach them to speak a few words, like parrots." Isn't it humiliating to think that out of the whole earth aviary, the only birds who can talk as we do are the raspy-voiced parrots and crows?

Do you know any way to stop their garden attacks? We all know that crows like to perch placidly on the heads and arms of scarecrows and are superbly scornful of rubber snakes and inflated plastic owls. They play with bits of cloth tied to wire fences and use metal pie plates clanking from tree limbs as looking glasses.

If it isn't enough that they make toys out of all of our defenses, my encyclopedia has to add, "The crow's diet varies with the time of year and the kinds of food available to him." Right on. Gardeners, we must all face the fact that that means the crow will quickly adapt its stomach to whatever we plant. If someday I manage to outsmart any crow, I promise to announce the triumph promptly.

---- ∘ 24 ∘ ----

Cauliflower

Tight, immaculate heads of snowy cauliflower have been an inspiration to some still-life artists. The trick for the gardener is to get the heads white and beautiful enough to pose for their portraits.

Let me admit that in our home garden, we don't always succeed. We've had years when some of the flowerets got so leggy and green they looked like broccoli side shoots. And we've had years when the heads turned yellowish, or developed brown spots from disease.

But we've learned. Last summer *all* our cauliflowers were gorgeous. They did mature all at once, which shortened the harvest season, but they were seed-catalog handsome. The plants made a sturdy row of fat green leaf-cups, each lovingly protecting a solid white sphere of crisp goodness.

Cauliflower is sensitive to anything that checks its steady

growth before it forms heads. Too much stress and the young plants form "buttons," or premature heads. Here are a few reminders to help keep your cauliflower crop stress-free. We followed these guidelines last summer, and they worked.

If you start plants in the warm environment of the indoors, be sure to harden them off before transplanting by putting them outdoors for just an hour or two the first day and increasing the time gradually, until they become accustomed to the sun and breezes.

Treat cauliflower roots very gently when you set plants out. If you buy transplants, choose ones that have been raised in separate cells so their roots won't be intertwined. We always set our cauliflower plants a bit deeper than they were in their original containers; that seems to help them regain their strength better after the move.

Cauliflower needs ample nitrogen throughout the growing season and consistent watering — no dry spells. I know gardeners get sick of hearing that advice, just as our kids get sick of being told to Be Careful! — but in both cases, the repetition reflects the importance of the advice. Finally, make sure your cauliflower plants don't have to compete with weeds for their meals.

While there are some warm-weather varieties, with most types the best cauliflower heads form when temperatures are no higher than sixty-five degrees; that's why some gardeners prefer a fall crop. They check the days to maturity, plan a September and October harvest, and count backwards to figure the appropriate planting day. In the cool days of autumn you won't have nearly as much trouble with insects, either.

To prevent direct sunlight from yellowing the cauliflower, blanch the newly formed heads when they're about three inches across. Blanch means bring some of the outer leaves together and tie them at the top, leaving ample growing room inside. Be sure heads are dry when you do this to avoid creating an environment for disease. Now and then, check the covered heads to see if they've matured; when past their peak they get a pebbly or "ricey" texture. Some self-blanching varieties form white curds without your help — their leaves naturally curl over the curds.

I like to serve crudités to guests because I can offer vegetables only an hour or so out of the good earth. White, foam-like chunks of cauliflower set off the brilliance of the carrots and cherry tomatoes on these platters. I was delighted to discover that youngsters who wouldn't touch cooked cauliflower with a ten-foot fork love crunching on crisp, raw chunks. That's great; they get all the vitamin A and C and potassium and we don't have to think up ways to encourage them to "eat all the nice vegetables, dear, they're so good for you."

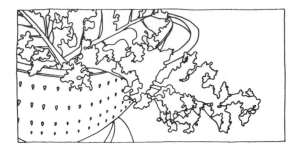

∘ 25 ∘

Try It. You May Like It

KALE

Start by eating kale because it's good for you, and you may end up eating it because it's good. For some people, it's an acquired taste. They admire kale's deep green, curly leaves garnishing meat and vegetable platters at fancy luncheon buffets, but think of it as a decoration, like parsley.

I'm a great eater of decorations. I love both kale and parsley and feel smug about it because both are rich in nutrients and low in calories. Kale is one of those vegetables, like collard greens, that offer a whole drugstore-full of good vitamins and minerals. A half cup of raw kale provides two-thirds of the recommended daily amount of vitamins A and C, a good thing to keep in mind when unexpected freezes in the South drive citrus prices into the stratosphere. It also contains potassium, calcium, protein, and iron and has only forty-five calories per cup.

To grow kale, sow seeds in the garden any time from early spring, as soon as the soil can be worked, through a few weeks before the last frost of fall. The leaves are beautiful; you can certainly plant kale in a flower bed. They're not as showy as flowering kale, which turns deep green with white, pink, or purple as it matures, but the edible kale plants stand tall for a handsome background to border flowers.

Gather leaves at will, working inward from the outside of the plant. Don't pick the terminal bud at the top center if you want leaves to keep coming. Try not to let leaves get really old; or if they do, pull those for the compost heap and gather the tender ones for the dinner plate. Old leaves get tough.

Kale will produce until the weather gets really cold. When nearly all the other garden plants have ended their season, there's summer-green kale tucked under the snows of November. And if you mulch the plants well, they may make it through the winter. Then you can enjoy a crop of tender young leaves in early spring before the plants go to seed.

SPINACH

"I say it's spinach and I say the hell with it," is an E. B. White phrase that's become a classic example of kids' reactions to some foods. Spinach did have a bad reputation a few years back. Too often it was boiled into a sloshy green mass that would turn off anybody's hunger switch. Popeye tried to give spinach good public relations, but he ate it out of a can. Canned spinach?

Real spinach is crisp, curly, dark green, and fresh, bearing no resemblance to its cooked version and far more enticing in salad than the pale iceberg lettuce. Spinach's biggest drawback as a garden vegetable is its stubbornness about temperature and day length. As the days get warmer and longer, spinach bolts and swiftly sets seed, and that's the end of it until the fall crop comes in.

At our house we get a long crop of spring spinach by planting an additional spring crop in autumn, just early enough to make a few leaves before heavy frost. In early spring when the weather is still overcoat-cool, our fall-planted spinach reappears and we enjoy the iron-rich leaves daily.

In midsummer, there's no *real* spinach in our garden. The stuff bolts so fast it isn't worth planting. Because we happen to like spinach steamed as well as raw, we grow New Zealand spinach (*Tetragonia tetragonioides*) for summer dining. In spite of its common name, it isn't spinach at all. Yet it has spinach flavor when cooked; and when I freeze it and use it in January, we truly can't tell the New Zealand from real frozen spinach. Pick the triangular leaves carefully from the long, trailing stems of New Zealand spinach; the stems are tough and bitter. It's good to harvest often, since the plant will go right on growing until the weather gets cold, by which time the fall spinach is ready.

One big advantage of our New Zealand spinach is that leaf miners don't attack it. We often get leaf miners in our spring spinach, though they don't go about their destructive work until the worst chill of early spring is gone; in the meantime, we have quite a bit of perfect spinach. Once the miners begin, all we can do is pull off the leaves they've been working on — often we can pinch out the brown parts and use the rest — and check *every day* for their eggs. Tiny leaf-miner maggots develop into equally tiny flies that lay their eggs in clusters on the undersides of spinach or beet leaves in spring, and they'll continue their damage as long as there's a leaf to work on. While I destroy any leaf-miner eggs that I find while gathering spinach, it would take far too long to check every single leaf each day, so the miners always win some battles. Some springs we find time to cover the plants carefully with fine netting so the flies can't lay eggs on them; that's the best control.

We have no special tricks or techniques for raising either standard or New Zealand spinach. Both crops are quite easy to start and require little care beyond watering. We plant them in compost-enriched soil with some fertilizer added to assure lots of green leaves, and that's it.

A bowlful of spinach leaves tossed with one or two chopped scallions and a light herb vinegar dressing takes about two minutes to make. It's just as delicious as far more complicated salads, it's high in nutrition, and it looks so inviting, I can't resist sampling it before it's served — sometimes to the point where I have to go out and pick more so there'll be plenty to go around.

PARSNIPS

Frost-tingled parsnips are so sweet and have such an unusual flavor, they can be used to enhance soup richness and cut the acidity of tomato-based stews and casseroles. Parsnips are slow growers, but I'm like the country philosopher who was told it would take him almost a year to grow a good beard: I don't begrudge me the time. There are two popular parsnip varieties: 'Hollow Crown' and 'Harris Model,' both yielding smooth white roots. It can take 175 days to develop decent-sized roots, but since you want them to grow well into the fall to develop their sugars, that isn't usually a problem.

Parsnip seeds take their own good time to germinate, so soak them for twenty-four hours before planting. Put them in an area that's clean of weeds, work the soil deeply so you'll get nice, straight roots, and stir in a good batch of aged manure. We mix radish seeds with the parsnip seeds; radishes germinate quickly and will mark the area where we have, in all likelihood, forgotten we put the parsnips. We harvest the radishes in plenty of time to provide adequate space for parsnips to fatten.

The blessing of parsnips, in addition to their special flavor, is that nothing seems to attack them. We've never had to worry about pests or disease, but we do try to keep the bed well watered so plants don't get woody. We also try to side-dress them once a month with compost and manure so they'll become sizable.

One year we didn't get around to thinning our parsnips to the recommended five inches apart, so we simply pulled some young ones and used them sliced in salads in August. That gave the ones we wanted to overwinter ample time and space to grow long and fat. Parsnips are best after a frost, and for their full sweetness to develop, they should stay in the ground all winter and be dug early the next spring. We mulch our parsnip bed under about two feet of hay in the fall, because we don't want the ground to get into a freeze-and-thaw cycle that might damage the plants.

In spring, we harvest parsnips as soon as the ground thaws. If we miss any and they start growing again, it doesn't take them long to get woody and tough.

The simplest way to cook and serve parsnips is also the one my family likes best. I peel the cream-colored roots with my carrot scraper and slice them into a sauté pan where I've heated a little butter. As soon as the slices are fork tender, we eat them; and I've learned to prepare what looks like an unreasonable amount for the number of people I'm serving, because calls for seconds are inevitable. If I want to dress up the dish for guests, I put some chopped walnuts or pecans in with the parsnips as they sauté.

Parsnips cook quickly. I add them to soups and casseroles only in the final twenty minutes or so of cooking time. Try putting some in whole with a pork or beef roast; they give the pan juices a wonderful flavor.

New Englanders, with their love for maple syrup, may want to try steaming chunked carrots and parsnips, about a cup and a half of each, together. Then doll them up with some toasted sesame seeds, a little salt, the juice of an orange, and two tablespoons of maple syrup. Let the whole works simmer until the liquid has been reduced to a glaze on the vegetables, and again be prepared to dish out second helpings.

CELERIAC

Every spring, I try to think of a few new plants to try in the vegetable garden — either completely new, or new varieties of old standbys. I read a lot of catalogs and books to find out the plants' ability to produce, the number of insect and disease problems they have, their tolerance for sometimes erratic care, their taste, even their appearance. If they meet all my standards with flying colors, there is still one last test they must pass before I'll plant them every year; my family must be willing to eat them regularly.

I can get my family to eat almost anything at least once; they're adventurous tasters, I'll grant them that. And they greet most of our garden bounty eagerly no matter how often it appears on the table. Nobody tires of luscious ripe tomatoes or tender sweet corn only minutes off the stalk. Still, there have been a few less common crops that merited only an "interesting; let's have it again in a month or two" response. We tried mustard greens and we tried okra, but for my family neither one passed the taste test. But when I started growing celeriac, bingo! We all love it.

Unlike its more familiar cousin, celery, celeriac produces a large, edible root that can be eaten raw or cooked. It tastes much like celery but is considerably easier to grow. It's also easier to store. It can be left in the ground until hard frosts come, then stored for several months in damp sand in a cool cellar.

Celeriac plants are hard to find in garden centers; you'll probably need to start your own. Give your crop an early start: sow the seeds indoors eight to twelve weeks before the last spring frost is expected. For example, I start my celeriac about Washington's Birthday. Gardeners in milder climates could sow seeds as early as New Year's. I sow about eight seeds in each small pot, eventually thinning to leave only the strongest seedling growing.

Like most root crops, celeriac does best in the garden if planted in well-prepared soil that's high in organic matter. I set the seedlings about a foot apart, spread mulch around them, keep them well watered throughout the season, and remove any side shoots that develop at the base.

As for insect and disease problems, we haven't had any so far, although I've read that wireworms, aphids, and slugs can cause minor trouble. Regular watering seems to me to be the major key to success; the one year I neglected to keep my celeriac well watered during a dry spell, the roots were woody and tasteless.

The first fall frosts arrive before I harvest celeriac; cold seems to improve the flavor. I usually let the roots reach three or four inches in diameter before I dig them; if they're much smaller than that, they hardly seem worth the effort after the peeling is done.

Celeriac leaves and stalks are quite handsome in the garden all season long, although they are too bitter to eat. But the roots won't win any beauty contests. They look sort of like hairy baseballs. When you peel away that dingy exterior, though, you'll discover invitingly crisp, ivory-colored flesh.

My favorite way to eat celeriac is in soups and stews. It

gives a delicate flavor to leek-and-potato soup, and makes a great addition to pot roast. Raw celeriac, cut into fine julienne strips and marinated for an hour or so in a mustard-yogurt dressing, makes an unusual and tasty salad.

So celeriac has passed all our family garden tests; it has earned its space in our garden.

RADISHES

Radishes aren't big news makers. They rarely move to the forefront of the human mind. Even some gardeners consider radishes merely quick-sprouting green tufts that mark where they planted the carrots. For many of us, the roots are only pretty little red globes that garnish the real food.

But most people just haven't explored the many radish possibilities. There are many more varieties besides those rosy globes and plenty of creative ways to spice up your cuisine with even the old standby varieties.

In the Orient the radish is a food staple. Not our common cherry-sized radishes, mind you, but carrot-sized or larger, slow-maturing winter radishes. They're usually planted in summer or fall and harvested in fall or winter.

They have lovely names — Sakurajima, Tokinashi, Miyashige. When you choose Oriental radishes, read the catalog or seed packet information about day length. Note that some radishes, like the daikon, need to grow when days are getting shorter. Don't plant them before late June.

Most winter radishes take from forty-five to seventy days to mature.

Black, pink, red, or white, these colorful vegetables are tasty raw or pickled, cooked alone or with other vegetables. Roll them in crumbs and fry them; slice and steam them; or put chunks of them in soups and stews. And of course, sliced thin, they're excellent in salads. These varieties put radishes right up there with the meat and potatoes — handsome, delicious vegetables to round out a full meal.

I'm not saying you should neglect the familiar spring radishes. Most of us haven't used them with much imagination. In France, young radishes are sliced and eaten raw atop fresh buttered French bread. Some gardeners who like their radishes *very* young and tender eat them stems, leaves, and all.

If radishes burn your taste buds, peel them; they'll be milder. Stir-frying and steaming also reduce their pungency. Or plant them quite early in spring, or in late summer, so they'll mature in cooler weather. Midsummer's radishes grow spicy with summer's heat.

A few gardeners, among them both the experimental and the negligent, have discovered one of radishes' best-kept secrets — radish pods. Radishes left too long in the ground, of course, become tough and woody. Left even longer, the plants shoot forth a flower spike that produces seed pods that look a bit like miniature sugar snap peas. In salads and stir-fry dishes their peppery crunch is a treat. Radish flower spikes bloom in sequence from bottom to top over several weeks. That means a long harvest, with several dozen pods from each plant. Young, crisp, bright green pods taste best, so pick them every three days or so.

Like the radishes from which they sprang, pods become mild when cooked. The trick is to give them just a minute or two of stir-frying or steaming. Don't let them overcook — they'll get dark and rather mushy.

Pods from all the spring radishes are good; try several varieties and see which you prefer.

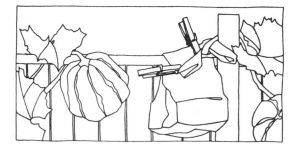

— ° 26 ° —

Bagging
Food Crops

More and more gardeners are deciding to bag it when it comes to trying to raise perfect fruits and vegetables. They're sick of having cucumber beetles gnaw on their melons and codling moths use their apples for boarding-houses.

So they get out paper bags, plastic bags, or — the latest thing — knee-high nylon stockings, and insert their produce in individual bags while it's still on the vine.

As with so many of our so-called new techniques, this one is old hat in other parts of the world. In Japan, some growers have used the bagging method of protection for years. They are able to command premium prices in the market for their bag-protected apples, pears, and melons. They need a good price; bagging takes time and patience.

The trick is to get the bags around the fruits early — as soon as the blossom closes and the little fruit starts forming. Of course if you're bagging fruits on full-size trees, you'll be able to wrap only the fruits you can reach. But that gives you an excellent means of comparison at the end of the season — you can see how the unbagged fruits compare with those you protected. Bagging forces you to do some helpful thinning, too; when fruits are too close together it's hard to get a bag on each one. The thinning helps assure there will be enough leaf growth to feed each growing fruit. Once you've tried bagging a few apples or melons for a season, you're likely to find yourself expanding the effort every year — it's such a treat to get pest-free fruits without using sprays.

Some gardeners use paper lunch bags over such fruits as grape clusters, which birds love to gobble for dessert. Gardeners in areas that get a lot of rain may find paper bags deteriorate too quickly; they often prefer plastic bags. Don't use paper bags on any fruits that rest on the ground; the bags will fall apart in damp soil. You can fasten any type of bag with either staples or clip clothespins. Snip off the two lower corners of the bags for air circulation.

An easy way to protect melons and squashes is to pull a knee-high nylon stocking over each fruit. Tie the toe to the top of the stocking after you've inserted the little fruit, and leave all the rest of the stretchy stocking for growing room. The mesh is so fine it keeps pests out.

Gardener Cathy White tested the stocking method in her Oklahoma City garden and proved that cucumber beetles can't penetrate the stocking mesh. She put beetles in a sack with stocking-protected squash, and none of the fruits were touched; she put other beetles in a sack with unprotected squash, and the bugs had a field day.

White reports she has tried both paper bags and knee-high stockings, and both work. She says she prefers the clip clothespin method of fastening the bags, because she likes to peek in now and then and see how growth is progressing.

Melons and squash that climb trellises bag up beautifully. You can close the top of the bag over one of the trellis wires and clip it shut with clothespins; or put the fruit into a knee-high and tie the stocking ends over the wire.

—o 27 o—

Saving Seeds

Why did my kids all inherit their dad's ultralong, hard-to-fit feet when they could so easily have inherited my ordinary ones? Why did they have to get my big ears instead of their dad's small, neat ones? Variations of these complaints can be heard from just about any parent. We often feel that nature, given a choice of genes for ears or noses or hands or feet, willfully selects the batch that will be the most annoying to the offspring.

Genetics works in mysterious and facinating ways. It usually takes beginning gardeners only about a year or so to want to dabble with seed saving. Next thing you know they're cross-pollinating plants with the devotion of Mendel and his peas.

Plant genes play tricks. That's why seed savers will find it at best amusing and mostly useless to save seed from any hybrid plant. Open-pollinated, or so-called standard varieties, run true to type; those are the seeds to save.

If you wish to save some of your garden seeds, bone up on what species sows seeds at what time, and learn which species need help with pollination.

Biennials (like cole crops, most root crops, hollyhocks, and foxgloves) don't set seed until the second year. To produce seed they must be hardy enough to get through the winter so they'll continue growing the next spring.

A prime seed savers' challenge is protecting plants from cross-pollination in order to get pure seed. There's little to worry about with beans, peas, tomatoes, peppers, eggplant, and lettuce, because they're largely self-pollinating. But don't save seed from cole crops, root crops, spinach, or any of the cucurbits unless you have just one variety in your garden — and as a matter of fact, none in your next-door neighbor's gardens.

There are at least three ways to prevent cross-pollination. Stagger plantings so different crop varieties flower at different times. Plant the different types well apart from each other, with a barrier of something really tall, like sunflowers, between them. Or protect the seeds of the chosen plants by covering them with cheesecloth or screening. Some crops need bees to pollinate their flowers — if you cover them you'll need to hand pollinate the blossoms.

Baby the plants whose seeds you want. Even if you can't keep up with all your garden demands, be sure those special plants get plenty of water, side-dressings, and protection from disease and insects. The healthier they are, the better their seeds are. Gather seeds from as many of these healthy plants as possible, and from several different fruits on each plant.

Cleaning seeds can be a job, but you don't have to get them as perfect as the commercial sellers do. You can clean many seeds by rubbing them over a piece of screening.

Choose a screen size that will allow the dirt and chaff to pass through. One way to clean wet, pulpy seeds like those of tomatoes is to puree the tomatoes in a blender with an equal amount of water. Then put the mixture in a bucket of water and wait for the seeds to fall to the bottom; pour off the water and spread the seeds on newspaper or paper plates to dry. Seeds must dry in a warm temperature, but not over ninety degrees; and air circulation is important.

When they're thoroughly dry, pack the seeds in silica gel for about a week, until they are completely dry and won't bend. Store them in airtight containers (those little black plastic camera-film canisters are ideal) and freeze them. When you take the seed containers out in spring, be sure to let them sit for twenty-four hours before opening the cans, so moisture in the air won't condense on them.

There's a thrill to saving your own seeds successfully. And if you have any heirloom plants no longer available through catalogs, you're also investing in the future — you are saving a plant variety that might, some day, be of benefit in plant-breeding work.

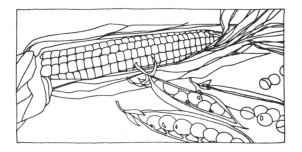

———○ 28 ○———

Harvest–
Picking at the Peak

In my hometown of Burlington, Vermont, it doesn't matter much whether I plant my vegetables in mid-May or the end of May. A few days don't make a great deal of difference.

Come harvest time, though, many vegetables have to be watched like cookies in the oven: there is one perfect time to pick, and if you miss it by a few days, you've lost some flavor, vitamins, and minerals.

Take peas for example. English peas and snow peas need to be picked when they're just at their peak of sweetness, because after that, whether on the vine or off, their sugars start turning to starch. Picking the pods from the vine speeds up that aging process, and your harvest goes from delectable to rejectable. Corn's the same way: you try to pick it at the peak of sweetness and eat or process it at once. That's why some gardeners prefer the new high-sugar corn varieties; they stay sweet longer.

Many vegetables give us vitamins A and C, some offer B-complex vitamins, and nearly all provide some minerals in the small amounts needed to keep us healthy. But vegetables lose vitamins just as they lose sugars: through delay in harvest, delay in processing, or overcooking. Even light makes a difference. For instance, the amount of vitamin C depends on how much light a plant has been exposed to, so a broccoli head grown in spring and summer is richer in vitamin C than one grown in fall. Tomatoes shaded by foliage have a third less vitamin C than those ripened in full sun. Even a few hours of bright sunshine can make a difference. So if there's a stretch of cloudy weather, it's worth delaying the harvest, if possible, until after a day of sunshine.

The B vitamins like thiamine, niacin, and riboflavin are highest in *new* shoots and leaves; carotene, the precursor of vitamin A, is highest in mature crops. Fully colored tomatoes, peppers, carrots, and dark leafy greens are all rich in carotene. The more intense the color, the higher the vitamin A concentration.

To protect both flavor and vitamin content in my vegetables, when any are ready to harvest and freeze, I get utensils in the kitchen prepared first. Then I pick the peas or beans or corn and get them processed and ready for the freezer before they know what hit them.

Many vitamins are concentrated in and just under the skins of fruits and vegetables. The less peeling and trimming we do, the more nutrients we save. Vitamins leach out in cooking water, too, so I steam or stir-fry most of our vegetables, whether fresh-picked or lifted from the freezer in midwinter.

At our house, many harvests are a family enterprise. Peas take forever to pick, they're so hard to find on the pea-green vines; and strawberries, beans, and other foods on low-growing plants can give the gardener that annoying affliction, "bean-picker's backache." So I often get my grandchildren, with their lithe bodies, to help with the harvest. Young kids have eagles' vision when it comes to spotting fresh strawberries or sweet peas on the vine, and if they eat some as they go along, they've earned them. In fact parents and grandparents are as likely as the smallest harvesters to munch as we pick. We don't even try to resist raw, sunwarmed, garden fresh fruits and veggies, just to have more for the freezer.

—∘ *29* ∘—

Putting Foods By

PICKLING CUKES

Crackling crisp cucumber pickles are the number one challenge faced by cooks who can their garden produce. Pickling is a ritual that calls for doing just the right thing every step of the way to ensure snappy results.

Any cucumber can be pickled, but it helps to start with a variety labeled "good for pickling" in the catalog or on the seed packet. Such varieties have the right texture and size for pickles.

Harvest the cucumbers as close to the time you're going to put them up as possible. When I can get my spouse or offspring to do the harvesting while I ready the kitchen for the job, I have a better chance of keeping all the cukes' moisture and flavor in from garden to jar.

I always sterilize canning jars the night before I'm going

to use them. I sweep the kitchen counters clean of the usual odds and ends that seem to collect on every flat surface in the Page house — books, newspapers, tape, hand cream, soap, condiments, sunglasses, outgoing mail, cereal boxes.

In the morning I lay out the spices and vinegar my pickle recipes call for, peel the garlic cloves, and gather fresh dill heads from the little garden beside our garage. Incidentally, for safe storage and crisp pickles, always use a vinegar of 4 to 6 percent acidity. (The vinegar-bottle label indicates acidity.) I usually use white vinegar because cider vinegar darkens the pickles.

When the harvesters bring in the cukes I scrub them and set aside any with doubtful spots on them. For dill pickles, and this also works for dilly beans, I put into each sterile quart jar one clove of garlic, a whole large head of fresh dill, and a teaspoon of mustard seed. And for each quart I boil together one tablespoon of pickling salt, two cups of water and one cup of vinegar. (Use an enamel, stainless steel, or glass pot for this, so the vinegar won't react with the metal.) While the mixture is coming to a boil I get my whole, small cukes packed into the jars, then pour the boiled mix over them. Yes, you can use regular long, fat cukes and slice them lengthwise, fitting the slices tightly into the jars; but my family thinks the crisp crunch is better maintained in whole cucumbers.

It's important to leave a half inch of head room in each quart jar and to put on the two-piece snap tops with the outer band twisted finger-tight. Then set the jars in a boiling water bath for fifteen minutes. Be sure the water covers the jars by at least an inch, and start timing when the bath starts to boil. A regular canning kettle makes the job easy, but I have also used an ordinary big pot with a tight lid and a rack set in its bottom for the jars to stand on. If you use pint jars, cut the ingredients per jar in half and process for just ten minutes.

I know that for years many cooks did not use a water bath

for pickles, just being careful to use sterile jars and boiling water so the lids would seal. However, it's been found that this method is *not* utterly reliable, and the government recommends that for our own safety and that of our families and guests, we use the boiling water bath.

I store the pickles for at least a few weeks in a cool, dark place to develop their flavor. Then I usually put a jar in the refrigerator overnight before serving the pickles. Their taste and crunch can upstage an ordinary hamburger, or hold their own in a gourmet sandwich creation.

FREEZING CORN

When my eldest daughter's child was a couple of months old, my husband and I went over one day to babysit. "Thanks, Mom," said our daughter, handing over Sara after one despairing glance at the crumb-strewn living room, "Boy, do I ever believe in the extended family!" When you've a job, a house, and a baby, it's impossible to have too many parents and grandparents, to say nothing of your sisters and your cousins and your aunts.

There's a time when *I* favor the extended family, too: when it's time to freeze the corn. I can shell peas or snap beans for freezing while watching television; but corn takes full concentration and, if left to one person, an awful lot of time.

As with cukes, what I like is to have my husband gather all the ripe ears from the garden while I scrub the kitchen sink thoroughly, set up the soup kettle for blanching the corn, open a few grocery bags for corn husks, and haul a big block of ice up from the downstairs freezer to put in the sink with plenty of cold water. I also put out two big cookie sheets where the pot-ready ears will be stacked.

Any and all are welcome to help shuck. Usually we have at least a husband and one daughter doing it. They shuck corn on the back step, warned by me that they'd better get all the silks off. I bring in the ears, six or eight at a time, rinse them under the spigot, and drop them into the boiling water, where they remain for two or three minutes depending on how young and tender they are. Then I lift them with tongs and put them in the sink, with its floating iceberg, to chill. Chilling corn ears takes time; I try to segregate the batches I lift out of the cooking pot by using the block of ice as a fence, but it's tricky because everything's floating. The only way to be sure an ear of corn is properly chilled is to hold it in your hand for ten seconds or so; if in that time you can't feel the heat from the cob, the ear's cool.

Then our other daughter, armed with a small, sharp knife and a huge pastry board, slices the kernels off the ears, being careful not to cut too deeply. When she has accumulated a good stack, I spoon the corn into pint freezer bags; press out the air; and seal, label, and freeze the bags. One of us runs down to the freezer every time there are a few pints ready and lays the bags as flat as possible, near the coils, so they'll freeze fast and keep their sweetness.

I've tried freezing corn on the cob and find it doesn't retain its flavor well and takes up a ridiculous amount of freezer space. Our off-the-cob corn is as sweet and tender in March as it was the day we put it up. If we're late in picking and any of the corn has gotten a bit old, I freeze that in separate packages and mark it for soup — a pint of corn added to vegetable soup adds color, crunch, and sweetness, and my soup cooks so many hours the corn gets tender even if it's old. Even then, it never seems as old as the fully mature, deep yellow kernels sold in grocery store cans and freezer packages.

Corn never makes as many pints as you think it will. A bushel may make five or six packets — but of course, mine contain more than a pint; I put in as much as possible, leaving only enough space to be sure of getting a tight seal. When the job is done, we haul out harvest baskets that look just as full of corncobs and husks as when we began. Those make good compost material.

DRYING FRUITS AND VEGETABLES

Our household never has gotten around to drying produce from the garden, but I'm beginning to think we're missing a bet, at least with some of our fruits and vegetables. Drying food saves time, storage space, and money.

Here's a space-saving example: twenty pounds of tomatoes will fit into eleven quart jars when canned; dried, they only weigh a pound and all fit into a single quart jar.

A good food dryer costs much less than a freezer, takes much less space, and uses far less electricity, because once it has dried the food you unplug it and put it away.

I'm not quite as convinced by the food-drying enthusiasts' claim that there is less work to drying. You have to steam most vegetables until they're very hot, as you would if you were going to freeze them, then put them into the dryer rather than into ice water. The slices drain and dry right on the dryer racks. However, steaming removes fewer vitamins than boiling, and you don't have to steam herbs or fruits at all, or such vegetables as tomatoes, peppers, onions, and celery. While any method of food processing causes some nutrient loss, a dehydrating guide tells you exactly which vegetable should be steamed before drying; if you're careful about steaming time, most nutrients will be preserved.

People who live in the Southwest can dry their food outdoors, but that isn't safe in parts of the country where you can't rely on full, steady sunshine and low humidity. Oven drying is possible but a bit tricky. If you really want to get into food drying, you're best off getting a commercial dehydrator. Margaret Gubin, an expert food dryer who teaches classes in the technique in Friesland, Wisconsin, told me it's important to choose a dehydrator with horizontal air-flow, to assure even temperature throughout the box of trays.

Arrange your chunks of steamed broccoli or slices of fresh tomato on the dehydrator shelves, in rows so they don't touch each other. Be sure to dry them thoroughly. Moisture left on them invites mold and fungus, and we get more than enough of that in the forgotten leftovers at the back of the refrigerator. Drying time takes from eight to twenty-four hours depending on your type of dehydrator and even on the weather. To test for dryness, take a few pieces out of the dehydrator to cool. Vegetables should be brittle and should snap, not bend, between your fingers; corn should be crackling hard; and fruits should be leathery but not sticky. If you're in doubt, dry them a little longer.

Rehydrating dried fruits or vegetables is easy. To add dried foods to soups or casseroles, just dump them in and they'll plump up, absorbing moisture as they cook. To use a dried food alone as a side dish, start with one part dried food and two parts water and simmer them, covered, for half an hour or so. If the water is all absorbed and the food still doesn't look plump enough, add a little more water. The important thing is not to start with too much water — you don't want to have mushy food, nor do you want to have to pour off any water; that way you lose nutrients.

Rely on common sense as well as printed instructions on drying. Test the dryness of each food for yourself, and be cautious about how much liquid you use to rehydrate.

Dried foods are nutritious, won't spoil if electricity fails, are easy to carry when traveling, and don't have to be watched while they're being processed. Children are fascinated by dried foods. They enjoy eating fruit leathers and dried fruit pieces, and watching dehydrated foods swell and freshen when water is added. Anything that helps kids enjoy good food is worth a try, in my book.

── ∘ 30 ∘ ──
Herbs and Potpourri

DRYING HERBS

Most of the old rituals for herb drying promoted by ancient herbal lore have been dropped. In some cultures, the honored herbalists had to gather medicinal herbs at night, naked, using no iron tools. The mosquitoes must have had a field day.

The ideal time to harvest herbs for drying is, in fact, a sunny morning, just after the dew has evaporated and before the sun has had a chance to reduce the oil content of the leaves. Handle herbs gently and gather them in small bundles so you won't bruise the soft leaves.

It is important to harvest your herbs at exactly their peak and to pick only the amount you can dry at once. Aromatic-leaved herbs like thyme, basil, oregano, sage, and others reach their peak when the buds are about to burst. If you want the flowering tops as well as the leaves, as you would with chamomile and yarrow, gather when the flowers are half open. Harvest lavender when the first flowers open and cut them with long stems, trimming the bushes at the same time.

If you want to dry only blossoms, gather them when they're fully out but just before they reach maturity. Handle these delicate flowers with great care. Pot marigold, rose, mullein, and German chamomile can all be dried, but they bruise easily. Wait until late fall to dig root herbs like horse-radish.

There are three requirements for herb drying, if you don't use a dehydrator: shade, a good current of air, and some warmth. You need shade because bright light draws the oils out of the leaves and bleaches them. Good air circulation is essential if you don't want to walk into the herb room and meet the musty smell that can occur in poorly vented cellars. Your carefully gathered herbs can turn limp and soggy. You want warmth so they'll dry to a crisp, crumbly stage as quickly as possible. If you can't supply the proper conditions, buy or borrow a food dehydrator.

The old-fashioned way — and some people still do this — is to hang bunches of herbs from strings, not touching each other, across an attic, outbuilding, dark barn, or shed where there is adequate air movement. You can hang a large harvest on strings hung from rafters or clothesline indoors.

You can dry some herbs in a microwave oven, though space is limited. Mints and basil will dry in three minutes; savory, rosemary, and thyme, with their small, dry leaves, need just one minute. Since not all microwaves are alike, it's a good idea to test just a few sprigs of any herb before drying your whole harvest.

No expert ever suggested my method, but it's worked for years with parsley: I put a bunch into the bottom of a paper bag far too large for it, blow air into the bag, and fasten the top tightly with a twist-tie and string. Then I just tie the string to a kitchen cupboard door-handle and the stuff dries beautifully. I've never tried this with my other herbs, but I bet it would work with mint, marjoram, and thyme, which are pretty easy to dry. If you try it, use just a small portion of your herb harvest until you find out whether it succeeds for you or not. I don't want to be responsible for misleading anyone about something you may rely on for favorite recipes.

POTPOURRI

Potpourri is summer to me. One whiff of a blend of roses, lavender, lemon balm, and mint with smidgens of such exotic additions as orris and I'm transported — even in winter — to a blooming flower garden.

Potpourris can be moist or dry. Moist ones are made from fresh flowers and leaves, layered with noniodized salt and aged and stirred and aged and layered again — all in a ritual that is more time-consuming than my gardening style. Granted, moist potpourris keep their fragrance longer than dry ones; some are said still to be fragrant after fifty years. They're not pretty, though — damp petals and leaves quickly turn into a wet mash. The word potpourri, in fact, comes from *pourrir*, French for "to rot." Moist potpourris are kept in jars that are, for obvious reasons, opaque. To release the heady scent of summer you close your eyes and lift the lid occasionally.

Dry potpourris are easier to make. Some carefully dried flowers and leaves can retain their color, too. Most people keep dried potpourris in glass jars, or make little sachets to tuck into drawers or drop into the bathwater. You can even put one in a pot of simmering water on the stove to give the kitchen — and the whole house — a delightful summery aura.

Most potpourris have a major scent, possibly a secondary scent, and a fixative to hold the fragrance. Classic flowers for the main scent are rose petals. The old-time gallica and damask roses are notable for strong rose fragrance. Lavender flowers, orange blossoms, and fragrant pinks are good too; they keep their color and fragrance as they dry. The secondary scent is usually light, to complement the main scent; it might be lemon balm, mint, bay, or scented geranium.

Orris root, made from the ground root of Florentine iris, is the fixative most commonly used to preserve your flowers' scent. It's available from most herb catalogs and shops.

To start a potpourri, pick flowers soon after the dew has evaporated on a summer morning. Dry them on a screen or newspaper in a warm spot out of direct sun, in an oven at its lowest temperature, in the microwave, or in silica gel — whichever you prefer — until they're crisp as cornflakes. Gather flowers all season, until you have enough for all the potpourri you want. Store dried flowers in an airtight container in a dark place until you need them.

Mix the flowers in pleasing proportions and add the fixative. (For orris root, use one tablespoon to each quart of petals.) Age the mix for three weeks in a covered jar in a dark place to develop the rich aroma. Next winter, on a dismal day when clouds threaten and the wind is howling, lift the lid of your potpourri jar and let yourself be carried back to sweet-smelling summer.

—— ∘ 31 ∘ ——

Bulbs for
Four Seasons

In the spring of 1986 our son-in-law went with his mother to the Netherlands to see the countryside when the tulips were in bloom. He was so carried away by the acres of brilliant color that he ordered massive numbers of bulbs as a gift for us, and some for his own household. We were thrilled.

Came the fall, and the bulbs arrived. My husband went out to the front of the house and doggedly hand dug a great big bed in which to plant the tulips. He turned the earth, gave it some rotted manure and compost, put a bit of bone meal at the bottom of each planting hole, and got them all planted. Next morning a third of them had been dug up by animals wanting the bone meal. We tucked the bulbs back into the ground, covered the whole area with chicken wire, and forgot about it.

The following spring, the display was staggering. The tulips were a rainbow, with colors from white to deepest red; some were so dark a purple as almost to deserve their description as "black tulips." Others were gentle pink and peach shades; some sported mixed colors; but all had that soldierly, confident, "look-at-me" air that sets tulips apart.

Not everyone receives such a generous gift or has the good fortune to go right to the source to order bulbs. Now that we're hooked on bulbs, we, like many gardeners, have found we've really had to do our homework before placing an order. We've learned that bulbs come in a wide range of quality and sizes in addition to an enormous selection of varieties.

When ordering any kind of bulb, from crocus to tulip (except daffodils), from an American catalog, look for ones labeled Topsize. "Topsize" designates the largest bulb in any species, so you know those will give a great splash of color. You may want to be cautious about a Topsize hyacinth, though. The bulb may be seventeen to nineteen centimeters (that's over seven inches) in circumference. You'll get a magnificent hyacinth, but even a little wind or rain may send it sprawling unless it's staked. About fifteen centimeters is a good size for hyacinth bulbs.

Be wary of catalogs that label bulbs "top quality" or "giant." Those words have no precise meaning. The word "giant" may be used the way cosmetics and perfume advertisers use it, as in "Buy the giant two-ounce size!"

When choosing tulip bulbs, you'll want to be aware of some special considerations. Surprisingly, there's a big difference between a Topsize tulip bulb and one only a single centimeter smaller. An eleven-centimeter tulip bulb is still in the growing stage. It will flower, but will not produce bulblets until the third year. The twelve-centimeter bulbs produce five or six bulblets the second year; or they may split and give you two elevens. In time, the original bulbs disintegrate and leave a group of small bulbs competing for space and food. That's why it's best to dig up and replant tulips every three or four years, or buy new ones.

The smallest tulip bulbs, smaller than six centimeters, are called "planting stock." These are bulblets that commercial growers grow out for several years, until they attain Topsize. Never buy planting stock unless you want three years of flowerless foliage; it may be five years before you get big, reliable flowers.

There *is* one tulip bargain: the intermediate-size bulbs called Premium. These are ten to twelve centimeters in circumference, a bit smaller than Topsize, and will give you a flower the first year; if the environment pleases them, they'll reach Topsize the next year. Premium size is usually what you get if you buy a mix of bulbs.

If you want to spend three years increasing your own stock of Topsize tulip bulbs, start with Topsize and at the end of the first year dig up the bulblets and replant them in some inconspicuous place. The next year each will produce a wide leaf; the second year you may get a small flower. The third year, you should get a colorful show of tulips from them, each one with prim, prissy stem and foliage and flamboyantly brilliant blossom.

Daffodils are a different story. One variety may produce bulbs two or three times larger than another, but each may have some characteristics you want. And then there's the matter of counting noses. Growers classify daffodil bulbs by both size and the number of growing points on each bulb — "noses." Each nose will flower the following year. So daffs are classified as DN-1, DN-2, or DN-3, depending on size and noses. Never mind exactly what the letters and numbers stand for — it's not what you'd guess. What's important is that the lower the number, the higher the quality.

The biggest, most mature bulb is a DN–1, with at least three and perhaps as many as five noses.

However, DN–1s aren't always the best bet. They're hard to find and expensive to ship. DN–2s give a perfectly good display in the garden, unless you're trying to produce show flowers for the county fair. Forget the DN–3s. Some companies offer *only* DN–3s, but each produces only one flower and will take several years to give you the same show as the DN–2s.

A few other tips on bulbs in general. First, don't wait till November or December to buy bulbs — by then you may as well stay home and wait until next season. The bulbs will be dried-out or soft and their nutrients will be used up. When buying any bulb, be sure it's sound — firm and crisp. The bottom should be white and hard, with no roots or shoots developing.

The brown skin or shell around a bulb, called the tunic, doesn't mean anything. Gardeners sometimes think a nice shell means good performance, but it's irrelevant. The shells split during drying and storage anyhow. If you buy bulbs without tunics, you can see whether they are either diseased or bruised; and they root faster without the shell.

What else should you watch for? If you're buying from a catalog, suspect any company that claims to have "blue tulips." There is no such thing, but apparently there have been cases where a company takes a photo of a pale lavender tulip, doctors it a bit, and calls it blue.

Although we often picture the large, showy flowers of tulips, daffodils, and hyacinths when we think spring, I'd recommend making room for a whole new category — the minor bulbs that symbolize the first days of the new season. Minor bulbs are little charmers that add subtle beauty to the landscape and invite closer looks. Most of them naturalize in good conditions and aren't bothered by pests or disease.

The snowdrop (*Galanthus nivalis*) is one of the earliest of the minor bulbs to bloom. It needs rich, well-drained soil and some shade. Its six-inch stems bear single, bell-shaped white flowers. Like most small bulbs, snowdrops are best planted in large drifts — and in this case, that fits their name.

Another lovely plant to try is glory-of-the-snow (*Chionodoxa luciliae*), which blooms with or slightly after the snowdrops. Delicate, star-shaped flowers are bright blue with white centers, and there are six to twelve blooms on each five- to eight-inch stem. They like light shade or full sun amid short grass, and they too will spread.

One of the most delicate looking of the minor bulbs is the giant snowflake (*Leucojum aestivum*). Clusters of white, bell-shaped flowers nod from two-foot-tall stalks. The tip of each petal is dotted with green. Snowflakes like shade, and bloom later in the spring than the others now namesakes.

Then there's the beautiful grape hyacinth (*Muscari*). Its clusters of tiny blossoms look just like upside-down clusters of grapes. Great drifts of deep blue-purple grape hyacinths under a blooming apple tree create a sight to make a poet out of a confirmed grouch. Grape hyacinths aren't fussy about soil; they like either full sun or partial shade; and they multiply and spread rapidly. You can get white and sky-blue varieties, too.

Siberian squills (*Scilla siberica* and *S. bifolia*) grow four to six inches tall, depending on the variety, and have beautiful blue flowers in clusters of three to eight. And one more favorite: the common or Dutch crocus (*Crocus vernus*) needs well-drained soil to produce those early harbingers of spring in white, gold, purple, or striped lavenders.

Early fall is the time to plant all these minor bulbs. Since they don't store as well as the big ones, like tulips, try to put them in the ground as soon as possible after you get them. The minors will give you a major treat next spring.

SUMMER

Once planted, spring bulbs (with the possible exception of tulips) remain underground to produce flowers year after year. The tender, summer-flowering bulbs must be dug up and replanted each year, but they are worth the trouble. Unlike annuals that die with frost, tender bulbs such as gladioli, tuberous-rooted begonias, and dahlias can be kept dormant over the winter for replanting the next spring.

I'm not botanically correct when I call all these things tender bulbs. Some, like tuberoses, grow from true bulbs; others, like dahlias and begonias, grow from tuberous roots; and gladioli grow from corms. As none of this affects your handling of these plants, however, I'll use "tender bulbs" as a handy way to refer to them.

Depending on the expert you talk to, you should dig up your tuberous-rooted begonias either when the foliage begins to yellow (but before the first frost) or immediately after frost has blackened the tops. I know gardeners who wait until after the frost, and their begonias don't seem to mind. In either case, leave the stems attached and keep as much soil around the tuberous roots as you can. Then cure (dry) them in a warm, well-ventilated spot for several weeks. When they're dry enough to store, the stems separate easily from the tuberous roots. Brush off any soil still clinging to the roots and pack them in dry vermiculite or perlite. Store them where the temperature will stay in the neighborhood of forty-five to fifty degrees — not always an easy neighborhood to provide, I know. Early next spring, when we're all squelching around in mud season, lift your spirits by potting the begonias. By the time warm weather arrives they'll be all ready to set out.

Gladioli are popular for the cutting garden; with their tall rainbow of spires they seem made to order for flower arrangements. Dig these corms when frost kills the tops, or when the foliage begins to yellow after flowering. Cut back the tops to within a half inch of the corm, then cure them for several weeks in a warm, well-ventilated place. You'll notice what look like the remains of an old corm at the base of the one you dug up; that's exactly what it is. Each year a new corm for the succeeding year forms above the old one; by the end of the growing season the old corm is withered. Pull it off and dump it. Glads should give you a bonus — there will be small cormels attached to the main corm. When the corm is dry enough to store, these cormels will separate easily from the larger one. You can save and plant them out next season, though you may not get flowers for a couple of years. Store gladiolus corms in paper or mesh bags in a dry spot with forty- to fifty-degree temperatures.

As with the begonias, whether to dig dahlias before or after the first frost depends on which expert you talk to. Cut back the tops of the dahlias before you dig them. Dahlia roots grow in a cluster; dig them carefully so you don't break any off. Handle with care — cuts and bruises invite disease organisms that lead to rotting. Once the roots are dug, dry them for just a few hours. They're tricky to store because they're sensitive to drying out. One recommended method is to put dahlia roots in a plastic bag with some barely moist peat moss or vermiculite, just enough to keep the roots from drying completely. If they're too moist, they'll start to rot. Dahlia roots like really chilly storage temperatures; thirty-five to fifty degrees would be best.

During the winter, check your stored tender bulbs now and then; remove any that show signs of rotting. And here's to a colorful, thrifty summer of bright flowers whose roots you rescued from a sure death in frozen earth.

AUTUMN

Stuart Robertson, a Canadian gardener, taught me a thing or two recently. In his column in the *Montreal Gazette,* he inspired me to think about planting autumn-blooming crocuses for a real change of scenery and a lift of spirit when I'm about to head toward one of those long Vermont winters. What a better way to announce the arrival of fall, just as spring crocuses proclaim spring.

Autumn-blooming crocuses (*Crocus speciosus*) look much like the spring crocuses with their narrow-bladed leaves and delicate, bell-like flowers in soft violet, pale blue, and white. They do best in sunny, well-drained spots, although *C. speciosus* is tolerant of damp soil.

For a conversation starter, there's *C. sativus* with its pretty, pale lilac blossoms and bright orange stigmas. The stigmas are the source of saffron, one of the most expensive spices you can buy. Fortunately just a pinch of it is enough to flavor and color a pound of rice. The stigmas can be gathered only by hand, and it takes about seventy-five thousand crocus stigmas to yield a pound of saffron; no wonder they are costly. In the Mediterranean region, there was a time when the theft of saffron bulbs was punishable by death. However, Robertson tells the story that a determined English gardener visiting the region filled his hollow walking stick with saffron bulbs. England being a country of gardeners, it didn't take these special crocuses long to spread.

There's another fall-blooming bulb, *Colchicum autumnale,* usually called autumn crocus or meadow saffron. It isn't a crocus, it isn't a saffron source, and it is poisonous. It's the source of a valuable drug called colchicine, used in gout treatment and plant hybridization. Colchicum flowers look a bit like crocus blooms, but the leaves are broader. Plants come in white, lavender, and several shades of pink.

Colchicum bulbs are expensive, about four dollars per bulb; but if you buy just a few, you'll find they spread rapidly, so your investment increases right before your eyes. They're a cinch to grow with sun and moist, well-drained soil. Robertson says he's had them arrive by mail with some flowers already showing; no matter, they can still be planted indoors or out.

These fall-blooming bulbs should be planted in late August, two to three inches deep and four inches apart. Set them in compost-filled holes or use a compost and peat moss mixture. Add a handful of superphosphate to help the roots grow. Water the planting mix well, and water again after covering the planted bulbs with topsoil. Cover the planting with thick mulch for the first couple of winters, until the bulbs have adapted to their new home.

WINTER

When it comes to cures for the long-winter blues, I've got two spring-bringers that I wouldn't be without. One is my annual visit to Florida relatives. The other is a sweet-scented pot of forced bulbs.

Some of the easiest to force are paperwhite narcissus. They're ideal for forcing because they don't have to live through a cold period before flowering, as must hardy bulbs like daffodils and tulips. Paperwhite narcissus blooms are borne in clusters and are so richly fragrant one potful can perfume an entire room. A yellow narcissus that's also easy to force is 'Soleil d'Or', "golden sun" narcissus.

Pot the bulbs in either pebbles or soil. Some gardeners claim they get better results with soil, but I haven't tried it so I can't substantiate that from personal experience. Pebbles are adequate since the bulbs contain all the food paperwhite narcissus need to bloom (and you're going to throw them away after the bloom anyway). Beautiful, fragrant, and no need for food? Heaven!

Leave the pointed ends of the bulbs just poking above the surface. Water the bulbs. If you use pebbles, water to just below, but not quite touching, the base of the bulbs; if you use soil, keep it barely moist. Then put the pot in a cool dark place for two weeks while the roots develop. After those two weeks, move the bulbs to a sunny window and give them two to three weeks to burst into bloom. That's all you do — no feedings, no pruning, no fuss. You can start a new potful of bulbs every couple of weeks during autumn, for a constant supply of flowers and fragrance from Christmas through ski season.

Forcing *hardy* bulbs is a little more work because you have to give them an ersatz winter. Daffodils, tulips, hyacinths, and crocuses need eight to fourteen weeks of exposure to temperatures between thirty-three and forty-five degrees; then when set in the sunshine they'll flower. The first step is to buy bulbs labeled as recommended for forcing. I've a friend who buys 'King Alfred' daffodils, pots them in a bulb pan filled with commercial potting soil, waters them, puts the pot in a ventilated plastic bag, and shoves it to the back of a refrigerator shelf. She makes sure the soil stays moist and in twelve to fourteen weeks hauls out the pot and puts it on a sunny windowsill. Sure, your family may grimace when in a hungry moment, they raid the refrigerator in search of something satisfying only to find bags of bulbs, but the bulb-forcing alternative is storage in a temperature-controlled root cellar or cool basement, or buried deep in loads of mulch outdoors. My friend likes early spring the easy way.

Every February, when the wind is howling and the snow's piling up, she can sit back and enjoy the potted springtime on her windowsill.

--- ∘ 32 ∘ ---

Extending the Season

FROST PROTECTION

Some years ago I met one of America's best-known gardeners, who had just finished working on a book that would give detailed information on how to keep a northern garden going late into the fall. I admired all he'd been doing. He chuckled and said, "Listen, I don't do all this stuff in our family garden. We start early in the spring and garden until frost, then forget it. We're glad to get the rest."

I guess I looked a bit shocked, since every devoted gardener is supposed to want as much of a twelve-month season as can be squeezed out. So he added, "Hey, if you have to fuss with the garden all year, when do you get a vacation? We take ours in winter and love it. We forget the garden completely. Then the next spring, gardening is a novelty again, and we can't wait to start planting."

Fair enough. I'm willing to admit that some people, especially those with so much garden they have trouble keeping up with it, like a break. But there are still plenty of us who want to keep things growing just as late into October and November as we possibly can, because our climate gets spring off to a late start in the first place. We learn how to help plants survive the early frosts of fall.

First, gardeners need to know their area's average first fall frost date; if a neighbor gardener doesn't know, the Cooperative Extension does. That date means there's a better than 50 percent chance of frost from that day on. After you live in a place for a time, you get to know the probable date in your own particular locality, which may be somewhat different from the frost maps. I also note the signs: a glorious blue and gold October day, when I can see for miles and feel the urge to sing a song or write a poem or just shriek with joy, may be what the old-timers call a weather breeder. The next day could bring a fall storm followed by a freeze. Also, still, clear nights with bright stars in mid- to late fall often mean there will be a silvery coat on the plants the next morning. Unusually warm days are often followed by frosty nights.

The handiest frost protections for the garden are row covers. Plastic tents or — the old standby at our house — retired bedspreads and sheets, secured by small logs or rocks, have helped many plants in our garden survive even several degrees of frost. Be sure covers are well anchored; you want them to trap the heat that rises from the earth in the night.

You can sometimes protect plants from frost if you start to water them before the temperature reaches freezing. Start sprinkling at, say, thirty-four degrees, and keep sprinkling until the sun melts the frost the next day. Ice will form on the plants, but as long as water is continually being applied, the temperature of the tissues won't go below thirty-two degrees. Many plants aren't injured until the temperature gets down to twenty-eight degrees or so. Both peppers and tomatoes may be saved this way. Delicate plants like squash and melons won't be helped, though. They are damaged by chilly air even when there isn't a frost.

At my house when frost threatens I try to preserve just a few rows of plants with covers. Often there's a warm spell after a frost, and we like to keep some of our garden vegetables growing — some years they get as much as another three weeks of warmth. We uproot tomatoes and hang them from nails in the garage while their remaining fruits ripen. If frost continues, at least we have the plants we've hung in the garage, plus the fruits we gathered and took indoors when frost threatened.

We rarely manage to have the earliest peas and greens on the block, but sometimes we can have tomatoes ripening outdoors when everyone else has given up. We don't brag about it, of course — at least, no more than we brag about our grandchildren.

FLOWER CUTTINGS

As the end of summer approaches, and nights begin to get a tingle of frost, I feel some regret as I look at my beautiful, soon to be frost-blackened flowers. The annuals, I know, would eventually come to the end of their short lives even if winter's cold weren't awaiting them. And the perennials will rest dormant under the snow, to blossom again next year. Still, I feel better if I can bring a bit of summer inside as the days grow shorter.

Perfect candidates for this are geraniums and many of the plants that grace hanging baskets: fuchsias, impatiens, begonias, and the like. They're all perennials and will keep growing, but are not hardy enough to make it through a cold winter outside.

My first instinct is to bring in the whole plant, but this

doesn't always work. Instead of a geranium covered with blossoms, I end up with a scraggly looking, leggy specimen with a couple of flowers wagging comically at its top. Perhaps if I had a greenhouse and could keep the geranium growing under ideal conditions, I'd have better luck. But in my house, winter plant visitors must share windowsill space with year-round-resident house plants.

The way to have vigorous carry-overs, I've found, is essentially to start with new plants — not by making a trip to the plant store, but by planning ahead and taking cuttings. In late August I round up my healthiest geraniums and cut off stem sections three to five inches long, trying to make the cut about a half inch below a node where a leaf is attached to the stem. I then strip off all but the top few leaves and remove any flowers. At this point, some gardeners recommend letting geranium cuttings sit exposed to the air overnight, so the cut end of the stem scabs over. I don't. I do dip the base of the cutting in rooting powder. (Some people skip this step, too, and still get good plants.) Then I stick the base of the cutting in a pot filled with moist vermiculite and cover the entire thing with a plastic bag. I have read that this is a no-no — the leaves may begin to rot in the moist environment — but, again, I've not had a problem with it and I think the cuttings root better in high humidity.

One thing I am careful about is keeping the pot out of direct sunlight; I don't want a cooked geranium.

Usually after a couple of weeks the cuttings have rooted and are ready to be potted in soil. The way to tell if your cuttings have rooted without digging them up is to tug ever so gently on them. If they're well rooted you'll feel the resistance of the roots holding them in the vermiculite. After your new plants get established and put on some new growth, pinch them back to encourage full, bushy plants to develop.

You can follow the same procedure with impatiens, begonias, and fuchsias. You may find your biggest hazard is propagating a lot more new plants than you have house room for. That's a good time to mend some social fences — nicely potted, healthy plants are charming gifts.

Next spring, you can take cuttings from the plants you started this fall and make a fresh batch of plants to put out in the garden. Not only is that a help to the plant and seed budget, it gives you a certain proud feeling, almost of parenthood, as you produce new young plants from aging ones. This kind of plant propagation can lead to a porch or terrace completely festooned with hanging baskets, and at very little cost except your labor, which you enjoyed, didn't you?

⸺ ∘ 33 ∘ ⸺

Closing Down the Garden

FALL CLEANUP

My mother was of the old school when it came to cleaning house. Every year she gave her house a spring cleaning in which every corner, every ceiling, every screen and sill was thoroughly washed. As if that weren't enough, she repeated most of the process in fall.

That's a level of cleanliness I'll never match — indoors, that is. But fall cleaning in the garden is another matter. If I don't wash ceilings and windowsills indoors in September, I don't have to fear the omission will invite disease and pests. But if I leave rotting cucumbers, diseased tomatoes, those strange spotty-looking melons we were afraid to use, and other spoilt produce in the garden over winter, I'm providing comfortable housing to disease-causing fungi, bacteria, and some larger organisms.

The most annoying job is getting rid of diseased fruits. Diseased leaves and stems will dry out quickly and can be burned, but burning a rotting cuke, which is mostly water, defies nature. On the other hand, we're afraid to compost these things because we aren't sure our compost piles always reach the 140-degree temperature needed to kill the dangerous organisms. So when something's really bad, I'm inclined to shove it into the rubbish. This goes to the local landfill. There it will be buried in an area containing plenty of helpful microorganisms that will destroy the fruit, eliminating the pathogens' food source.

Some experts say tilling under diseased plants in the garden can work the same way. I'm just not brave enough to try it with fruits that look as if they've really been clobbered.

We weed both in and around the vegetable garden in fall, too. Tilling is a big help, but there are always some perennial weed roots that accept this as an opportunity to multiply; luckily, they're not hard to dig out. Weeds around the garden can harbor disease and insects that will become an attack army by next spring.

Then we plant a cover crop; buckwheat, which grows thickly and crowds out weeds; or a legume like hairy vetch (*Vicia villosa*), which adds nitrogen to the soil. Buckwheat really has to be planted in very early fall, though, to make any useful growth.

One year we covered one of our gardens with a deep blanket of hay and leaves instead of planting a cover crop, and I must say it made spring planting easy. We just pushed the mulch aside to start our vegetables in spring.

Unfortunately, the number of slugs we attracted that summer dampened our enthusiasm for the mulching system, so I'm not sure we're ready to try it again. We also had more earwigs than I've ever seen before; they love dark, damp, rotting material like the lower layers of our mulch. I dubbed this the Year of the Earwig. We had beautiful lettuce that spring and summer, but I had to wash it leaf by leaf to get all the earwigs out. They didn't eat it — they were just hiding in the crevices, seeking dark and moisture. Their preferred food is spoiled or rotting plant material. They probably ate the lower level of mulch, which was OK with us.

One more fall chore at my house this year will be to get a soil test, as we haven't had one for a few years. The best time to add lime and other soil amendments is in fall, since most take a while to benefit the soil. Fall cleanup is one form of insurance for a bountiful garden next year.

WINTERIZING THE GARDEN

The last three pumpkins are sitting on the front steps; all the rest have gone to various children or have been baked and their contents frozen, as I've nowhere to store the big fruit. The lawn is raked and the vegetable gardens have been cleaned up and planted with cover crops. Is it time to relax and gloat over the produce-filled freezer? Not quite. Our various young trees and shrubs like their share of TLC before winter's cold seeps into their bones.

First we make sure they've had enough water; trees and shrubs in dry soil can be winter-injured. They want moist, not soggy, soil, so most years we give everything a good drink before the ground freezes. Evergreens especially need this — they lose moisture through their needles all winter long.

Mulch is good winter protection, but we have learned by experience not to put it down too early. That can interfere with the plants' natural development of cold hardiness in response to the shorter, cooler days of fall. In fact, gardeners who mulch under trees and shrubs in summer would be wise to pull the mulch away from the trunks in late August. Don't push it back until hard frosts threaten. We mulch young shrubs in November to keep soil temperature warmer and allow root growth to continue later into fall.

Although we also mulch the flower garden, we don't do it to keep the soil warm. There, our aim is to be sure the perennials stay safely frozen all winter long. What they can't stand is alternately freezing and thawing when our unpredictable winters start their yo-yo exercises on the outdoor thermometer. Young or newly divided plants are most susceptible to this kind of injury; frost heaves could expose their roots.

Snow is a welcome mulch for flowers. Unfortunately, we can't rely on it staying all winter, so we use hay too. We don't use leaves, as all but oak leaves are likely to mat and smother plants. We don't mulch perennials early either. When they're completely dormant and we know the ground is frozen, usually sometime in mid-November, we start doling out armfuls of hay from the garden cart.

There's no way we can blanket our tall evergreens. Some of these can suffer leaf scorch from winter wind and sun. The broad-leaved evergreens are most susceptible, and for these, prevention's the best protection. Plant rhododendrons in protected locations with a north or east exposure. If yours are already planted elsewhere, try antidesiccant spray from the garden center. Applied on a mild day in late fall, it helps reduce water loss from plant leaves. Some ambitious gardeners actually build protective structures around vulnerable trees and shrubs, but the structures look pretty weird all winter long, and they're a lot of work. I think it's better to put the plants in a protected spot to start with.

Like babies with delicate skin, young trees have tender bark prone to winter sunscald and frost cracking. That happens when the bark on the south side of the tree is heated by sun reflected off snow, then chilled when the sun sets or is hidden by clouds. The bark may be split or even killed. Protecting the trunks of young trees with tree wrap tape helps reduce this kind of injury. And cages of metal mesh around the bottom of the trunk keep the rabbits and other creatures from feasting on tender bark when snows make food scarce. In the past we had a young tree actually killed by rabbits and mice eating its bark in winter; the deep snow allowed them to reach surprisingly high.

When all the mulching and watering are done, you can relax with the satisfaction of knowing that as your plants mature they won't need so much cosseting. Then there will be no excuse to postpone cleaning the garage so the car will fit in it during winter.

——◦ 34 ◦——
The Value
of Trees

Like most gardeners, our family has planted trees, both evergreens for landscape improvement and fruit trees for consumption (much of the latter by fruit worms). But we've
never done, or helped with, any large-scale tree planting,
even though we rejoice every time such work is undertaken
by anyone. The value of trees in holding soil and water and
cleaning the air can hardly be exaggerated, I believe. I'd like
all gardeners to be tree groupies.

I had a lovely time recently rereading Dorothy Canfield
Fisher's account in a 1949 *Vermont Life* magazine of how
she and her husband planted thousands of trees on their
property in Arlington, Vermont. She explains that they put
in the huge future forest at least in part as an act of con-
science: it was the author's folks who had destroyed the
fine old trees on and at the foot of Red Mountain, and she

felt "that the traditional American love for our rocks and rills might well show itself not only in singing about them but by taking a little more care of them."

Photographs show the barren landscape the Fishers started with, the thriving young woods ten years later, and ultimately the superb full-grown forests that developed between 1914 and the 1940s.

We have four stubby little pines, quite out of place in the tiny garden beside our garage, stuck there "temporarily" four years ago when they came free with another tree order. When new, they looked hopeless, and I think when we heeled them in in our kitchen garden we suspected they'd never make it; but we couldn't bring ourselves to throw away any living thing that had potential usefulness.

Our pines are still in their infancy — but they're a few inches taller, much fatter, and healthily green, and one tug proves they have tenacious roots. Apparently in their first few years pines are always slow. Ms. Fisher wrote of hers, "those minute specks of green seemed to stand still." Like ours, they were mere tufts of needles about as big as a toothbrush.

Once a young pine gains confidence, though, it grows with the enthusiasm of a would-be basketball player. By the tenth year, the Fishers had a fine adolescent pine forest; by the twentieth, they had forty-foot towers of green. That means we *must* make a decision about our four little pines no later than next spring, before they start their upward growth spurt. Already they look ridiculous in the little kitchen garden of herbs, lettuces, and tomatoes, though so far visitors have politely refrained from comment.

The place to put our pines is on poor, thin soil, where almost nothing else will grow. Pines will grab such soil in their rooty hands, hang on for dear life, absorb rain and sunshine, and thrive to become giants, making a nice bed of needles at their feet.

As the author says in her magazine article, it seems impossible for so small a human effort to produce such a huge effect. Even the ten thousand trees she and her family planted the first year (and they did it all themselves, with the help of a couple of neighbors) cost only fifty dollars — not much, even back then — and two days' work. With that small investment, they have given Vermont a whole new forest, produced usable timber, and beautified both a mountainside and the heretofore barren pasture at its feet.

Our four pines can't do all that, but now more than ever, I want to find an appropriate place to let them live and thrive.

─── ∘ 35 ∘ ───

The Gardener Indoors

VOILÀ VIOLETS

My friend Sal loves her flowering plants so much that she caters to their every whim, watching each one with a mother's eye. She obviously considers her house plants part of the family; and thanks to that attitude and care, everything she grows thrives. So she's the person I went to when I first considered raising African violets.

She has a dozen of them in shades of pink, violet, deep purple, and white, some with single circles of petals, some as frilly and delicate as foaming lace. "I've never bought an African violet," Sal told me. "I started them all from leaf cuttings from friends. It's the easiest thing in the world." She warned me the big danger was that I'd find myself so caught up in the fun of multiplying these plants — getting something for nothing, so to speak — that I'd end up in a kind of violet jungle.

To get started, all you need is a mother plant, a sharp knife or razor, and a container filled with some light potting soil or vermiculite; a commercial African violet mix works well. Select leaves from the crown of the plant — those from the outer edge don't root as readily — and cut them with a one- to two-inch leafstalk.

Some garden books recommend letting the cut leaves sit for several hours or overnight. The idea is that the cut end can heal somewhat and lessen the chance of rot. Other people dispense with this step and have no problems; it's amazing how durable the cut leaves are. In fact, African violet enthusiasts often exchange plants by sending each other leaves through the mail. They wrap a bit of moisture-retaining material around the leafstalk and seal the whole leaf in a plastic bag. Spring and fall are the best for long-distance swaps — summer heat and winter cold may damage cuttings.

When you are ready to stick the leaf cuttings into the potting mix, dampen the mix and make holes in it with a pencil. Then poke the leafstalks into the holes at a forty-five-degree angle until about three-quarters of each stalk is covered. Enclose the whole pot in a plastic bag, making sure the plastic doesn't touch the leaves. If necessary, prop up the bag with a piece of wire or some old popsicle sticks. Put your pot of leaves in a spot with bright light, but out of direct sun. After about a week, leave the bag open a bit to allow the air to circulate.

In about a month you'll see plantlets springing up from the base of the leafstalk, your signal to remove the plastic covering.

Because so many plantlets form, divide them before they get too big. When they're about an inch high, carefully dig up the clumps, cut off the parent leaf, and separate the baby plants; set each in its own two-inch pot. Then for the better part of a year, all you have to do is water them and feed them one-quarter-strength house-plant fertilizer monthly. Repot them when they need larger quarters. In about ten months, your African violets will bloom. Line them up on a bank of shelves, mix the colors to please your taste, and voilà. You've a ready source of pleasure for the family, and gifts for friends.

EASY AS AMARYLLIS

I admire gardeners who thrive on challenge. They're the ones who grow the prima donnas of the plant world, those that insist on exacting, meticulous care or they'll slouch, fade, and die. Some gardeners get plants to grow in inhospitable climates, or make them bloom at a time of year when the plant's every instinct is for an extended nap time. I admire these dedicated gardeners, but I'm not tempted to compete in their world.

Sure, I like some challenges too — like producing really early tomatoes, or outwitting the raccoons near the corn patch. But when it comes to house plants, I feel there's been challenge enough by the time I find correctly sized flowerpots and the right potting mix to put the begonias in. I want a plant that doesn't need constant care, isn't too finicky about temperature, and looks handsome when the neighbors drop in.

There's one absolutely spectacular flower I grow indoors that almost never demands service. Amaryllis (*Hippeastrum*) rewards casual care with a breathtaking burst of bloom atop a thick two-foot stalk, year after year. The amaryllis bulb is dramatic, too. It's the size of a small grapefruit, making even a big tulip bulb look seriously underfed.

Amaryllis flowers range from bold scarlet (my favorite) through pink and salmon to white and even bicolors.

The bulbs usually flower six to eight weeks after they're potted up. For a succession of bloom through the winter, pot them up at intervals from midfall through December. Deck the halls with at least one pot of bright red amaryllis in bloom for Christmas. You get a lot of color from just one plant: they stay in bloom for three or four weeks, especially if your house is on the cool side, and some send up a second stalk of the huge, lilylike flowers.

The big bulbs are not claustrophobic; they *like* tight spaces. Put an amaryllis bulb in a pot just an inch or an inch and a half greater in diameter than the bulb at its widest point. Set the bulb so its top half is above the soil line. Water thoroughly, then don't water again till you see new growth beginning. Some amaryllis shoot up flower stalks very quickly, others take their time. Some produce the flower stalks first, others start by sending up their swordlike leaves. They are happy at normal home temperatures, but try to give the flowerpot a quarter turn every few days so the stalks won't end up all bent out of shape from reaching for the light. Amaryllises need at least a half day of sun.

To keep an amaryllis from year to year, leave the plant in its sunny spot after it's finished blooming and continue to water and fertilize it; the green leaves store food in the bulb for next year. When the leaves yellow, cut them back, stop watering and fertilizing, and let the bulb rest in a coolish place for at least a month; two or three months won't hurt, if it's more convenient.

When it's time for the bulbs to start growing again, you usually don't need to repot them; do so only if it's clearly necessary. Most amaryllises produce fine blooms for three years in the same pot. Just wash away the top inch or two of soil in the original pot, add fresh soil, and start the cycle again.

I wish all recycling were as easy — and as rewarding.

THE GARDENIA AND THE SPIDER MITES

Gardenias make me think of jitterbugging. Their fragrance carries me back to my college years in the 1940s. At that time, when you had a dance date you could be pretty sure your corsage would be gardenias, and the dance was always the jitterbug.

So when a friend surprised me with a gardenia plant one gloomy winter day, I was so pleased I forgot one of my cardinal house-plant rules: *quarantine* all new arrivals for a few weeks to see if anything catching shows up. One whiff of that heady fragrance, a glance at those succulent white blooms, and I gleefully put the gardenia right in the big window with my other plants.

Oops! How could I do that?

After a couple of weeks on my windowsill, my gardenia began to look a little peaked; the leaves began to turn a mottled yellow. With a sinking feeling I got out the magnifying glass. Sure enough, the gardenia was infested with spider mites — and so were the neighboring plants, and it was my own fault.

Spider mites are insidious and tenacious. Tiny, too — one-fiftieth of an inch or less. Unless you're very sharp-eyed, you probably won't be able to see them. The mottled and browning foliage may be your first sign of their attack. Spider mites suck plants' juices, slurping up the chlorophyll that plants need to manufacture food. As you look closely, you may see a network of fine cobwebs on the undersides of leaves. One check for spider mites is to put a sheet of white paper under a plant and tap on the foliage. If dustlike specks fall on the paper, you've met mites.

Spider mites aren't true insects. They're more closely related to spiders with their eight legs. The type most commonly found on house plants is the two-spotted spider mite (*Tetranychus urticae*).

Like so many pest bugs, mites reproduce like crazy. With the right temperature and humidity, mites can go through the whole cycle from egg through three molts to adult in as little as a week. A female can lay over a hundred eggs in her short lifetime. If there isn't a male mite handy, she lays eggs anyhow. Unfertilized eggs become males; fertilized eggs become females. And diet is never a problem for this clan — they'll suck on just about any plant.

Pesticides often aren't much use. Mites produce so many generations, so fast, and in such huge numbers, they develop pesticide resistance quickly. What can we do? Washing plants off regularly with strong streams of water can send mites at all stages of their life cycle down the drain. Insecticidal soap sprays help; repeat the spraying at least three times, at weekly intervals.

Sometimes all efforts are hopeless. I had to throw away my lovely gardenia. I bought a new one, examined it carefully, and kept it in quarantine for three weeks before I put it with the other plants.

I'll probably never be able to say I have a pest-free outdoor garden, but by gosh I'm determined to keep pests out of the plants that perk up my home.

CHRISTMAS CACTUS

Near an office where I once worked, there was a small-town bank that I loved to visit. The manager there had a green thumb that didn't come from handling money. He had spectacular orchids in the bank's front windows, and the biggest Christmas cactus I've ever seen in a south-facing window at the rear of the building. It was growing in one of those enormous metal laundry tubs our grandmothers used to use. It bloomed magnificently and regularly: each Christmas it was covered with pink blossoms whose petals curved back in tiers to reveal sprays of delicate anthers. The banker told me that he had inherited the huge plant from his grandmother, and that he kept it at the bank because there wasn't proper space for it at home.

A few people who visited the bank had the treat of being accompanied to the back room, not for special loans (the room's nominal purpose) but to see the gorgeous cactus.

Christmas cactus (*Schlumbergera bridgesii*) has a close relative (*S. truncata*), commonly called Thanksgiving cactus because it blooms a few weeks earlier, and a slightly more distant cousin, Easter cactus (*Rhipsalidopsis gaertneri*). The care of all of these holiday cacti is the same.

Christmas cacti are not desert dwellers, not by a long shot. They're native to the rain forests of South America, and are what is termed epiphytic cacti. That means they grow in trees, not on the ground; their roots are anchored in organic matter that collects in the crotches where the trees branch. That explains why they don't look very cactusy — they don't need prickly spines to protect themselves.

During the rain forest's dry season, Christmas cacti go through a resting period before setting flower buds. To get them to flower at home, gardeners must mimic those conditions and give the plants a rest when cooler temperatures and shorter days prevail. To create an artificial dry season, gradually reduce the plant's water intake, starting about mid-September and continuing for eight weeks. To simulate cool night temperatures, find a room in the house, possibly an unheated space, where night temperatures are in the fifties.

A friend who has done this successfully reported to me that after resting in a cool room, her plant set flower buds regardless of day length. If you don't have a cool spot, however, you can get the plant to flower by manipulating day length. Give the cactus thirteen to fifteen hours of uninterrupted darkness every night for eight weeks. You could stick it in a closet at 5:00 P.M. and take it out at eight the next morning; just don't forget the poor thing. And don't forget that opening the door or turning on the light for even a few seconds cancels the long "night."

Even easier for those in USDA Zones 5 or cooler, set the Christmas cactus outside in a shady, protected spot for the summer and leave it out until frost threatens. By the time you bring it in, it will usually have been exposed to enough cool nights to set buds.

Apart from the need for a rest, Christmas cacti are easy to grow. They like bright light, constantly moist soil, and monthly feeding with half-strength house-plant fertilizer from the time the flower buds appear until the fall rest period. They flower best when somewhat pot-bound, so you needn't repot often. Best of all, as with the one in the bank, they are remarkably long-lived, getting bigger and better as time passes. The only real problem with one of these heirloom plants is finding a big enough pot and broad enough space to keep it in. If you can get one started with your children and grandchildren in mind, introduce them to its needs now. Then that living antique can brighten their lives for many years.

——— ° 36 ° ———

Winter Scenes

Looking out at our garden covered with snow, its raised beds like ancient gravemarkers, I sighed to a visiting neighbor, "Gosh, Susan, I wish spring would come so we could get a little life back into the garden."

"Come with me," she said. "I'll show you something." Anything would look better than that scene. We headed for her house. Inside we viewed her garden from her back windows.

I was instantly envious. Each of her windows framed a picture worthy of a still-life artist's brush. In one corner of the yard, bright coral-red twigs of Siberian dogwood (*Cornus alba* 'Sibirica') made startlingly lovely exclamation points against the white snow. In the opposite corner, punctuation was provided by the black stems of the common winterberry (*Ilex verticillata*), with dangling bright red fruits. Evergreens lined one side of the yard. Birds were everywhere, darting about to snap up the shining berries, or chattering away in the evergreens.

I decided then and there it's more important to have a fine winter scene than a summer one. In summer gardeners may occasionally sit on a lawn chair to sip a lemonade, but not for long. All around are dozens of tasks crying to be done — carrots to weed, greens to mulch, hedges to trim — so you end up gulping the lemonade and grabbing a hoe. But in winter you can enjoy the view. Fix a hot chocolate or tea and relax in an easy chair near the picture window, admiring your snow-pure yard.

I'm sold on the idea. Now, what do I plant? My neighbor suggests starting as she did, with the Siberian dogwood — it's the most civilized of the shrub dogwoods. Its cousin isn't a bad choice either; the red-osier dogwood (*C. sericea*) spreads by underground stems to form a thicket. Both reach about six feet in height. They have small white or bluish white flowers in early summer, and creamy berries that attract birds in fall. For gardeners who prefer sunny colors, there is a dogwood called goldentwig (*C. sericea* 'Flaviramea') that has bright yellow stems.

Winterberry, a deciduous member of the holly family, is another good choice. It grows well in soil too wet for some other plants, but is adaptable and will grow in drier soil. Its glowing red berries remain on the shrubs long after the cold and snow have settled in. Berries not only brighten your picture, they're an excellent source of food for many birds. Like all hollies, winterberry bears male and female flowers on separate plants, so buy at least one male plant to pollinate the others.

Trees as well as shrubs add sparkle to the winter scene. My helpful neighbor recommends crabapples, especially Red Jade crab (*Malux* 'Red Jade'), which has pendulous branches that sweep to the ground in graceful curtsies. The small scarlet fruits remain on the tree well into winter. On a fine snowy morning your Red Jade crab will look like a delicate Japanese painting, framed by your window.

Take time to think about these special plants. Browse through catalogs, talk with neighbor gardeners, and look for winter-pretty plants around town. In future winters, your back-yard scene could be alive with color and motion outdoors, even though indoors you'll be strictly still life, sitting cup in hand admiring it all.

ABOUT THE NATIONAL
GARDENING ASSOCIATION

The National Gardening Association is a nonprofit, member-supported association of two hundred thousand of America's most devoted gardeners. NGA is dedicated to helping people garden successfully at home, in community groups, and in schools and institutions, because we believe gardening adds joy and health to living while improving the environment and encouraging an appreciation for the proper stewardship of the earth.

National Gardening Association members receive *National Gardening,* a full-color monthly magazine. Each issue includes advice on growing America's favorite fruits, vegetables, herbs, and flowers; tips from gardeners coast to coast; the latest research on new seed varieties; and pest control and work-saving techniques. NGA members can also tap expert advice through the Gardening Answer Service.

NGA's radio program, *The Gardening Journal* with Ruth Page, gets advice, information, tips, and anecdotes out to gardening listeners nationwide via the public radio system.

Books are an important part of the National Gardening Association's informational services. Among our books in print are *Gardening: The Complete Guide to Growing America's Favorite Fruits and Vegetables, Gardeners' Questions Answered, The Youth Gardening Book,* and

Grow Lab: A Complete Guide to Gardening in the Classroom. Also produced is the *Yardening* series, our twelve-volume set of gardening videos.

Other activities of the National Gardening Association include the *National Gardening Survey,* an annual report produced in cooperation with the Gallup organization, surveying gardening trends for the nation's media and the lawn and garden industry; Grow Lab, funded by the National Science Foundation, a hands-on indoor gardening program for teaching science in the classroom which includes an indoor gardening unit, curriculum, teacher's newsletter, and training videos; and the National Gardening Grants program and Green Medal Awards, which provide seeds, garden tools, and information nationally to youth programs and schools.

For a sample copy of *National Gardening* and information on how to join the National Gardening Association, write to the National Gardening Association, Dept GJ, 180 Flynn Avenue, Burlington, Vermont 05401.